THE ART OF DINING OUT

Howard Hillman

How to: select the ideal restaurant
• get full value for your money • assert your rights
• judge the food • order wine
• get the best table • receive VIP treatment

POCKET ℗ 46196·6·$5.95

Why Should You Never Eat Chinese Food on a Monday?

Monday is the traditional day off for the number-one Chinese chef!

AND MORE FASCINATING FACTS . . .

- Sampling wine is a ceremony that stems from centuries past—to prove to suspecting dinner guests that the wine was not poisoned.
- When a butter-fingered waiter spilled coffee on Dorothy Parker's designer gown, the great wit allegedly quipped, "Go and never darken my Dior again."

In Howard Hillman's witty, informative insider's guide to dining out, you'll learn:

- how to tell if a restaurant serves glorified TV dinners
- how to judge the food—including how to tell fresh from canned pâté
- how to dine in special situations—from entertaining a client to romancing a lover
- how to know the right wine to order, and how to pick wine bargains

AND . . .

Beware of typographical menu errors that slipped by the proofreader, such as "Our chef's own brains sautéed in butter."

YOU'LL ENJOY EXCELLENT MEALS
WITH SUPERB SERVICE—
AND MAKE YOUR DINING
DOLLARS COUNT—WITH . . .
THE ART OF DINING OUT

THE ART OF DINING OUT

Howard Hillman

Editorial Assistant: Soneni Bryant

PUBLISHED BY POCKET BOOKS NEW YORK

An *Original* publication of POCKET BOOKS

POCKET BOOKS, a division of Simon & Schuster, Inc.
1230 Avenue of the Americas, New York, N.Y 10020

ISBN: 0-671-46196-6

First Pocket Books printing April, 1984

10 9 8 7 6 5 4 3 2 1

Design by Stanley Drate

Contents

INTRODUCTION   9

1

SELECTING THE RESTAURANT   11

   Timing / 13
   Deceptive Reviews / 14
   Advertisements / 16
   Fame / 17
   Value / 17
   Glorified TV Dinners / 18
   Continental Cuisine / 19
   Decor / 19
   Window Displays / 20
   Entertainment / 20
   Other Selection Factors / 20

2

GETTING VIP TREATMENT   23

   Cultivating a Restaurant / 25
   Telephoning for Reservations / 26
   Reservation Ploys / 28
   Complying with the Dress Code / 29
   Identifying Who's Who in the Dining Room / 30
   Identifying Who's Who in the Kitchen / 32
   Waiting for a Table / 33
   Obtaining a Good Table / 34
   The Human Factor / 36

3

ORDERING THE FOOD   37

Menu Fraud and Hype / 39
Oral Menus / 44
The Credibility of the Waiter / 45
Plan Ahead / 46
Who Places the Order / 47
What Not to Order / 47
Be Adventurous / 49
Ask, Ask, Ask / 49
'Tis the Season for Asparagus / 50
The Chili Immunity Factor / 51
Gastronomic Pyromania / 52
Gastronomic Machoism / 52

4

CHOOSING THE BEVERAGE   53

Wine / 55
Wine Pronunciation Guide / 61
Beer / 69
Cocktails / 70
Drinker's Lexicon / 71
Nonalcoholic Beverages / 79

5

EATING THE MEAL   81

Table Etiquette / 83
Identifying Silverware and Glassware / 89
Establishing Rapport and Your Credentials / 89
Pet Peeves / 92
Lodging Complaints / 94
Toasts / 95

6

JUDGING THE FOOD 97

A Sensual Primer / 99
What to Look For / 100
Other Pointers / 105
Counterfeit Ethnic Fare / 108

7

MAKING THE GRAND EXIT 111

The Check / 113
Competing for the Check / 114
Tips on Tipping / 114
Credit Cards / 118
Paying With Cash / 118
Penniless / 118
Doggy Bags / 118
A Restaurant's Liability / 119

8

COPING WITH SPECIAL SITUATIONS 121

Entertaining Business Clients / 123
Eating on the Road / 127
Traveling Abroad / 130
Dining Alone / 133
Dieting in Restaurants / 134
Feasting on a Shoestring / 136
Bringing the Kids / 138
Amusing Your Visiting Aunt Rhoda / 140
Hosting a Foreign Visitor / 140
Romancing a Lover / 141
Brunching in Style / 143
Going to the Theater / 144

Being a Dinner Guest / 144
Attending Formal Banquets / 145
Enduring Institutional Food / 147
Dealing with MSG Maniacs / 147
Saving a Choking Victim / 148

9

TRANSLATING FRENCH AND ITALIAN MENUS   151

French Menu Translator / 153
Italian Menu Translator / 163

10

POTPOURRI   173

What's a Gourmet? / 175
Are the Pleasures of the Table Sinful? / 176
Exposing Food and Wine Snobs / 178
The "Pierre Must Be an Authority" Myth / 182
So You Want to Be a Restaurant Critic / 183
Don't Envy a Restaurant Chef / 185
The Pitfalls of Owning a Restaurant / 186
How Sanitary Is Your Favorite Haunt? / 187
Fast Foods / 187
A Peek at the Future / 190

ABOUT THE AUTHOR   191

Introduction

Dining-out savvy is an essential tool in today's business world. You must be able to deal with and take total command of the booby-trapped restaurant-going ritual whenever you take a client or a colleague to lunch or dinner. Your career may even depend on it, because major decisions are often made at a restaurant table.

My book will help you gain the needed expertise, quickly and simply. It will give you an invaluable competitive edge.

The tips and insights that I share with you are not only important for your business success, they will also help you acquire an enviable social grace. You will be able to dine with self-confidence in any type of restaurant, from the family-style eatery to the *haute cuisine* temple.

The Art of Dining Out will also help you get your dollar's worth in this day of escalating prices. Some of my pointers can save you in a single meal many times the price of this book.

Perhaps the ultimate benefit of this handy volume is that you will have more fun dining out. The whole process will take on new and exciting dimensions that you probably never dreamed existed. Dining connoisseurship is one of the most satisfying of hobbies.

It is also one of the most practical, because you spend a fair portion of your life at restaurant tables, more than you might imagine. Did you know that more than one hundred million Americans eat at least one of their meals away from home on a typical day?

For your benefit, I have organized each of the ten parts of this book into quick-reference sections. This format should save you time in finding the particular information you need.

The insider advice I share with you is based upon my combined years of experience as a restaurant critic, food and wine author, gastronomic lecturer, cook, waiter, bartender—and even busboy, dishwasher, and potato peeler.

Here's but a sampling of the hundreds of gutsy tips and behind-the-scene insights that you will learn:

—how to get the best table
—how to spot menu frauds and hype
—how to test and either accept or reject a wine
—how to avoid etiquette blunders
—how to critique the food
—how to tip the captain
—how to impress a client
—how to romance a lover
—how to pronounce French menu terms
—how to deal with snobs

As you can see, there is more to the art of dining out than most people realize. And the more you know, the richer your dining experiences will be. That's why I wrote this book for you.

Bon appétit!

HOWARD HILLMAN

1

Selecting the Restaurant

Choosing a restaurant is much like sex—not all of us are willing to admit that we could benefit by learning more about the act. For instance, do you know why Monday is generally the worst day to eat in a Chinese restaurant? Why Sunday is usually not the ideal day for eating fish? Why Saturday night is an inopportune time for enjoying a skyline view?

TIMING

Never eat Chinese food on a Monday, unless you know who is manning the wok. Quality in a Chinese restaurant will usually suffer because Monday is the traditional day off for the number-one chef. Since the normal day off for chefs in other types of restaurants can be either Sunday or Monday, get into the habit of asking, "Will your top chef be on duty?" whenever you are making a reservation for those days.

Sunday is not the best day for ordering fish, because few restaurants receive fresh deliveries on Sunday. The problem with Friday in a seafood house is the crush of people—most of us still associate fish eating with that day.

Don't go to a restaurant on Saturday or Sunday night for its skyline view. Instead, visit on a workday evening, Monday through Friday, when lights of office buildings are kept lit for the cleaning crews. The vista then is at its breathtaking best.

Midday Friday is not the perfect time to eat in a moderate-to-high-price restaurant in a business district. These eateries are particularly packed because Friday is payday for many companies. Nonmanagement personnel often choose that day to splurge some of their earnings for a fancy lunch with friends and office mates. Should Friday fall on the first or fifteenth (the usual semi-monthly pay dates), the lunch scene will be even more crowded.

Forget about having lunch on matinee days in a theater district like New York's. Most of the restaurants are saturated with the unappetizing din of bus groups of prating theatergoers.

Friday and Saturday are the busiest dining-out nights. Sunday afternoon can be hectic, too, in suburban family-oriented restaurants. Unless you have a firm reservation that will be honored on time, you risk getting indigestion from waiting for your table.

Oddly enough, foul weather is not necessarily undesirable for a

13

restaurant-goer. The fact that you, unlike many others, decided to show up tends to make the chef and waiters more obliging. Moreover, since rain or snow keeps more patrons than employees away, the staff-to-customer ratio improves in your favor.

Consider the time of day. If you plan to eat during the lull hours, between lunch and dinner, ask the restaurateur whether the key chefs will be working or taking a break. In the latter case, the range will be tended by a fledgling cook who will be literally learning at your expense.

Should you be planning to be one of the first customers for lunch, you'd best be certain of the restaurant's standards. It is possible that your five-dollar hamburger might be cooked with ground beef left over from last night (or from days before if the restaurant was closed yesterday).

When you want to eat a late lunch or dinner, pick a restaurant that does an active business during those hours. I always find it disconcerting to be told that the kitchen has run out of dishes I want—or to be eating while waiters are stripping tablecloths from nearby tables.

There are a few instances when peak hours are the only times to visit a restaurant. Suppose you want to have prime rib in a steakhouse that features that specialty. By placing your order when the dining room is bustling, you increase the odds that your meat will be cut from a freshly roasted rib section.

Shun a brand-new restaurant. You are better off waiting at least a couple of weeks until an eatery has completed its shakedown period. When an operation is still in its embryonic stage, it usually has gremlins to catch in its newly installed equipment, relationships to develop among a hodgepodge of food suppliers, and waiters and kitchen help to train.

I would also be cautious of a restaurant that has just received a rave review. Delay your visit for two or three weeks after the review hits the newsstands. Until then, there will probably be long lines creating a flurry that disrupts the rhythm and undermines the proficiency of the kitchen and the patience of the dining-room personnel.

DECEPTIVE REVIEWS

The Finnish composer Jean Sibelius opined, "Disregard what critics say. A statue has never been erected to any one of them."

Sibelius's derisive judgment holds true for some of my fellow restaurant critics.

The disservice these critics perpetrate is that they mislead you into spending your hard-earned dollars in unsuitable restaurants. The best defense against being victimized by reviews is to know the many ways in which they may be flawed. Let's examine these potential defects, one by one.

Some reviews are bought. In exchange for a glowing write-up the restaurateur gives the "critic" a free meal or signs an advertising contract with the publisher. If the establishment refuses the offer, it gets no review, regardless of its culinary merits.

One clue to payola reviews is that they are grossly uncritical and often effusive. The Pollyanna prose overflows with glowing accounts but conveniently overlooks shortcomings (even the best restaurants in the world are not perfect).

If you have doubts about the impartiality of a newspaper or magazine, call or write its editor and ask point-blank whether it pays for its critic's meals and whether the critic's opinions are independent of the influence of the advertising department. Draw your own conclusions if you receive an evasive answer.

When evaluating the evenhandedness of a dining-out guidebook, look for the written guarantee that the author refuses freebies. For the record, some of these authors accept complimentary meals.

Even upright critics can lack objectivity. For instance, there are those who wear French-colored glasses. They seldom study the myriad of cooking styles that originate beyond the borders of France, and consequently their reviews tend to judge other cuisines with the French set of culinary values. Cream sauces, thyme, and wine are not *de rigueur* for a great cuisine.

There are those critics who announce their presence when they enter a restaurant, yet claim they can still accurately assess the food and service despite their blown cover. Horsefeathers. When restaurateurs know someone is reviewing their operation, they provide better service. They also select the best cut of meat and instruct their chefs to take extra care in preparing the order. If they didn't, they would certainly be foolish entrepreneurs.

Don't take a restaurant critic's authority at face value, as many of them are gastronomic dilettantes. Competent critics need a thorough understanding of the principles of cooking, whether they learn it in a home or restaurant kitchen. Those who tell you they can properly judge the incredible variety of traditional and new dishes without having this culinary mastery are either fooling you or fooling themselves.

Distrust any critic who opts for the cleverly written phrase at the expense of hard facts and sound judgment. This grandstanding is endemic in restaurant-review journalism. In their zeal to grab the spotlight from their fellow reviewers, these critics often go to one of two extremes: being predictably venomous or giving away more stars than are in the firmament ("on a scale of ten, I bestow eleven stars on Stella's Pizza Joint").

I know of one critic who seems to think of himself as an undiscovered literary genius. He wants to write *The Great American Novel,* but over a dozen book publishers have rejected his manuscript. In his frustration, he uses his restaurant reviews to show off his literary skills. Inevitably, what his reviews lack in depth they make up in length.

Then there is a new breed of restaurant critics: those who appear on local television news shows. I admire their charismatic on-camera personalities. Nevertheless, an amusing reviewer who lacks gastronomic expertise should be labeled an entertainer rather than a critic, and the value of his or her counsel should be weighed in that context.

Check the date of any review you see in a restaurant window. Reviews are perishable, since a restaurant could have a new owner or chef. Also look for the copyright date of restaurant guidebooks, as some volumes can best be described as history books. Unfortunately, seeing the current year in the copyright notice is not full assurance that the reviews are up to date. Some of the entries may have been based on visits made several years earlier.

Ever wish that you could be a reviewer? Before you succumb to that urge, be sure to read the section entitled "So You Want to Be a Restaurant Critic" on pp. 183–85 in Part Ten, "Potpourri."

ADVERTISEMENTS

Promotional advertisements are seldom reliable guideposts for selecting restaurants. Most of the eateries that do a lot of advertising are saying, in effect, that they find it more profitable to spend money attracting a steady stream of new customers than to spend money pleasing customers sitting at the tables. If a restaurant is good, then it generally needs to advertise only during its first year of operation. After that, the establishment should be able to keep tables filled by means of repeat business and the favorable word of mouth generated by the satisfied customers. When a good restaurant does advertise after year one, the ad is usually low-keyed and institutional in nature.

FAME

Contrary to popular opinion, fame does not equate with quality—more than three-quarters of America's best-known restaurants serve mediocre food. Some of these gastronomic duds are living on the reputations of their once-glorious kitchens. Others gained their renown because of their megabuck advertising budgets and their well-financed publicity programs. Yet others gained their prominence through a fluke such as exposure through a hit movie.

Sometimes it is the chef's fame rather than the restaurant's that is the magnet. Even if the chef is as good as his or her billing, make sure the luminary is still toiling behind the swinging kitchen doors. Normally, chefs quit or are fired from their posts without public notice.

Many diners erroneously reason that if a waiting line is long, the food must be fabulous. Experience has taught me that one rarely finds excellent meals in restaurants that repeatedly have extensive queues. People who know and appreciate fine food seldom have the patience to stand in lines for lengthy periods, even for top-star fare.

VALUE

Restaurants that specialize in crêpes, soups, or salads seldom offer the remarkable value that some diners attribute to them. Though their prices are relatively low, these establishments sell a specialty that requires little culinary skill and costs only a small amount of money to produce. The stuffing for the $6.95 Crêpe Neptune, for instance, was probably precooked, frozen, thawed, and reheated. Even the inexpensive crêpe batter probably was purchased frozen by the restaurant. (And these eateries encourage a fast customer turnover.)

For long-term value, you should aim for a memorable dining experience. I have spent moderate sums for countless humdrum meals in mediocre restaurants that I have long forgotten. I have also paid a hundred dollars for meals in gastronomic nirvanas that brought me sheer pleasure that I will be reminiscing about in years to come.

Value, of course, is relative to one's own financial state. During my scrimping student days I would never label any restaurant a value if its meals cost more than fifteen dollars, no matter how splendid the food was. At the same time, however, I was never impressed with a bargain-priced, gargantuan portion of sirloin steak if the meat was mediocre or improperly cooked.

GLORIFIED TV DINNERS

Avoid restaurants that serve entrées that have been frozen, thawed, and reheated. This process robs meats, fruits, and vegetables of too much of their desirable flavor and texture.

Lamentably, more than 50 percent of the moderate-price restaurants in metropolitan areas serve at least a few frozen packaged items. Few waiters will admit this practice, but, fortunately, a menu can give you a clue to whether an establishment's cuisine is dominated by frozen foods. It probably is if its bill of fare features a number of items that happen to be on the restaurant industry's best-seller list of frozen entrées. These dishes include:

Baked Clams Casino
Beef Wellington
Breaded Chicken Breast
Breaded Fillet of Sole
Breaded Shrimp
Chicken Kiev
Chicken or Veal Cordon Bleu
Coquilles St.-Jacques
Deviled Crab
Guinea Fowl or Cornish Hens
Lobster Fra Diavolo
Lobster or Seafood Newburg
Spinach Soufflé
Veal Parmigiana

Stuffed anything—including crêpes, peppers, and poultry—are also prime suspects. So are casseroles, stews, and ground-meat preparations—as well as almost any food served hidden under a thick, heavy sauce. Even prime ribs of beef sometimes spend a lengthy respite in the freezer. "Fresh food" all too often signifies that the delicacy has come fresh from the freezer. Entrées that are the least likely to be frozen are grilled and sautéed dishes.

CONTINENTAL CUISINE

Boycott restaurants that feature Continental cuisine—the fare is bland and predictable. It was invented at the turn of the century by Swiss hoteliers who needed a "safe" cuisine to suit the motley palates of their guests, who came from all corners of the European continent. Though this hybrid creation borrows heavily from the French and Northern Italian styles, it remains a compromise cuisine, with all the attendant woes that befall solutions designed to please everyone. As *New Yorker* writer Calvin Trillin quipped, any restaurant that says it serves this style of cooking probably has the continent of Australia or a transcontinental bus company in mind.

DECOR

Steer clear of those restaurants that cater to people who eat primarily with their eyes rather than with their senses of smell and taste. These enterprises often have the recipe for financial success but rarely for good food. They do everything to keep your mind off their inferior culinary offerings.

You know the ilk of restaurant I'm talking about. The lighting is so dim you need a flashlight to examine the food and read the menu, which is written in cornball English. The decor is bizarre and kitschy, and a clone of other eateries throughout the country. The waiters wear outfits rejected by central casting.

On the other hand, I'm not advocating spartan dining environments. I, too, like something pleasant to look at during a meal: tasteful furnishings with a touch of the restaurateur's personality. It is a matter of aesthetics.

WINDOW DISPLAYS

Ever see a bottle of wine bathing in the outdoor light as it sits in the window of the restaurant? If it is a dummy (that is, empty) bottle of wine, the proprietor is conscientious. If it is an unopened bottle, the wine will surely develop an off flavor. Most proprietors who display wines in a window eventually serve them to unsuspecting customers.

Also be chary of eye-catching displays of fresh meats, fruits, and vegetables. Restaurateurs usually display their choicest ingredients and cook with the rest. When the display items eventually become tired and withered, into the kitchen they go.

One of the newest hypes in the restaurant world is to dress fresh-faced employees in chef's smocks and *toques blanches* and have them intermittently make a batch of flat noodles with a hand-cranked pasta machine. When they're not in the window doing one of their brief showman's stints, you can see some pasta strands protruding between the meshed grooves of the machine's dormant rollers. Few passersby would suspect that in most of these establishments virtually all the pasta that is served inside the restaurant is purchased from a commercial pasta-making firm miles away. Your odds of getting any of the token amount of pasta that was produced on the premises are thinner than capellini.

ENTERTAINMENT

Quality food and entertainment—be it a big-name singer or disco music—are usually mutually exclusive. To help defray the high cost of these musical offerings, restaurateurs must sharply cut corners in the kitchen. If you must eat at the entertainment spot, stick to those items that are least likely to be botched by the chef (salads or sandwiches, for instance).

OTHER SELECTION FACTORS

To make the best of all possible decisions, you should also take into account these issues: Is it too late to make a reservation for the desired time and date? Does the restaurant fit your mood and occasion? Is the dress code compatible with what you plan to wear? If you are pressed for time, will you get the prompt service you need? If you want to dine leisurely, will the restaurant try to rush you? Is the food too spicy or too bland for your taste? Is the restaurant geographically convenient? Is parking available and reasonable? Is the neighborhood safe from crime?

Maybe you want to select a restaurant for a business client, child, lover, or visiting relative. You will find tips and insights on these topics and more in Part Eight, "Coping with Special Situations."

2

Getting VIP Treatment

Who doesn't relish receiving VIP treatment in a restaurant? Once you learn the velvet ropes, you can enjoy the red carpet normally unrolled for ambassadors, movie stars, and captains of industry.

Hard-to-get reservations will become available. Maître d's, bartenders, and waiters will greet you with a smile and the sweetest words in the English language, your name. You will be escorted to choice tables and be offered daily specials the hoi polloi will never know. Your requests will be handled with respect and dispatch. This reception cannot but impress your guests.

CULTIVATING A RESTAURANT

The surest way of getting VIP treatment, short of being a celebrity or the owner's mother, is to become a regular. A quality restaurant must give special services to its steady customers if the management hopes to sustain their loyalty.

Regulars are important to the success of a restaurant because they are the best fountain of favorable word-of-mouth publicity. They also tend to be bigger spenders than now-and-then patrons. (When the glutton Diamond Jim Brady died, the owner of one of his favorite restaurants lamented, "I've lost my four best customers.")

If your business or social needs require the cultivation of dining establishments, this section will explain how to make the right moves. The methods are tried and proven.

Rule number one: You must curtail your gastronomic promiscuity. You do not have to give up philandering altogether, but you should concentrate on a small but well-rounded list of restaurants tailored to your needs. For an executive in Manhattan who frequently entertains clients, a basic list might include these categories: French (both an *haute cuisine* temple and an informal bistro), Northern Italian, Chinese, Japanese, Seafood, and American Steakhouse.

Whatever the number of restaurants you have under cultivation, you must frequent the establishments enough to be a familiar face. If you haven't had the opportunity to eat in one of your pet spots for the past two or three weeks, consider stopping in for a quick afternoon drink to refresh your whistle and relationships.

Suppose you have visited a restaurant for the first time and wish to cultivate it. The best approach is to get a regular at the restaurant to introduce you to the management. (See the section

"Identifying Who's Who in the Dining Room" starting on pp. 30–32.) If you do not have a contact, then try discreetly giving the maître d' five or ten dollars on your way out. Tell the maître d' that you enjoyed dining in his or her establishment and would like to make reservations for a choice table on such-and-such date in the near future. You can be almost certain that on your next visit you will be greeted by name and assigned a better-than-average table. Repeat this cycle until you become part of the well-entrenched clan.

Be cultivating the other staffers, too. If you are satisfied with your captain, specifically request to sit in his or her area whenever you make reservations. The captain will be flattered.

Occasionally send a pleasant but pertinent compliment to the chef on the back of your business card. Before long, the chef will probably make a special trip from the kitchen to your table, a sign that you are now a full-fledged regular. Thereafter, periodically send the chef a small gift: cuff links, earrings, or twenty to fifty dollars in cash.

Sometimes it is the little thoughtful gestures to the staff that count as much as or more than money. Should you vacation in Portofino, drop them a picture postcard.

TELEPHONING FOR RESERVATIONS

Usually it is best to call a day or two ahead of time. If the day and restaurant are very popular, a week or two in advance may be advisable. Reservations have a way of inadvertently getting lost or scratched off the list, so reconfirm on the day of your visit. Reconfirming also freshly imprints your name in the mind of the maître d'.

Telephone during meal hours. Often the person answering the phone before or after the lunch or dinner period is not the official reservation taker. Busboys and subordinates have a propensity for distorting reservation requests or forgetting to pass them along.

Some restaurants deny they take reservations but, in truth, do. They will give them to their regulars, to friends of regulars, and to individuals who seem to be the type of clientele they are trying to attract.

Be confident. Don't ask for a reservation—state it. Briefly deliver your request in a firm but civil voice:

I would like a good table for two at 8:00 P.M. this Friday. The name is Mr. Hodges.

Notice that the request is made for a *good* table. This petition costs nothing, does no harm, and sometimes gets results.

Keep a list of the owners and maître d's of the restaurants you wish to visit again. Your chances of getting a reservation at the last minute are vastly improved if you can say, "Hello, Robert, I would . . ."

On your first sojourn at the restaurant, build the maître d's confidence in you by asking a few knowledgeable questions about the menu. For instance, inquire if the veal comes from milk-fed calves.

Should the restaurant have a special off-the-menu meal or dish, consider ordering it ahead of time. In many cases, the incremental cost is negligible—and you'll probably receive VIP treatment when you arrive. Expect the same reception when you tell the maître d' that the occasion is very special to you. Few restaurateurs are so hardened that they won't pamper you a little on, let's say, your tenth wedding anniversary.

If you want to order one of the restaurant's specialties and you will be arriving near the end of the meal period, ask the maître d' on the telephone to save a portion for you. Usually the management will comply.

Anyone whose name is regularly garbled by reservation takers should adopt a simpler, sure-to-be-understood alias. The Kolodziejs of this world might wish to use Cole when calling in their reservations. This tactic might insult their ancestors, but it will help the living Kolodziejs get the table they reserve.

We get angry when a restaurant doesn't honor our reservations. Why shouldn't a restaurateur feel the same way when we don't live up to our end of the bargain? Cancel your reservation as soon as you know that you are not going. Also alert the restaurant if there will be a change in your arrival time or in the size of your party. Your thoughtful deed gives the management the information it needs to devise an efficient seating schedule. It also enables the maître d' to tell another patron, "Yes, I can confirm you for a table of four at nine o'clock," instead of saying, "I can't promise you anything, but if you come by at nine, I'll see what I can do."

RESERVATION PLOYS

Scheming diners have bags of clever tricks for securing difficult-to-come-by reservations. Let's examine some of their subterfuges.

The great pretender casually mentions on the telephone that he's been to the restaurant many times before and relies on the reasonable assumption that a restaurateur has so many names to remember that he can't recall them all. If our schemer learned of the maître d's name in a newspaper article, he confidently lets it roll off his tongue as if the maître d' were his old crony. The counterfeit reinforces his bogus credentials by enunciating his name in a matter-of-fact way that insinuates that the maître d' would be a dolt not to know the identity of the caller. The phony might also add, "Give me the same type of excellent table that you gave me last time." If he is unfamiliar with the layout of the restaurant and the maître d' should ask him, "Which table did you have last time, monsieur?" the mountebank promptly hangs up and hopes for better success with the next restaurant on his list.

Another deceiver's tactic is to fake a long-distance phone call: "I'm in London and will be arriving on the Concorde today. Won't you please hold a table for me at nine o'clock tonight." The reservation taker, who is often impressed by this sort of humbug, doesn't realize that the caller is a short subway ride away.

Yet another favorite ruse is for callers to request the name and vintage of the restaurant's most expensive wine. Upon hearing the response, frauds say, "We might just try that wine with dinner tomorrow night. Can you arrange a table for us at eight?" Once they are ensconced at the table and the sommelier asks, "Shall I bring you the bottle of 1955 Château Petrus?" the impostors change their minds: "We've decided to try that wine on our next visit. For tonight, a carafe of your house red will do." Price difference: $416.

Occasionally the reservation-making con artists bestow on themselves the title of Doctor, hoping to score points with the restaurateur. The restaurateur knows that M.D.'s usually spend more than nonphysicians and might be more inclined to offer a reservation. But there is a frequently overlooked pitfall in using this artifice: it could backfire someday. Imagine the maître d' coming over to your table and whispering, "Please follow me, Doctor. The customer in the powder room is about to give birth."

Some ploys take place at the maître d's reservation stand. How many times have you overheard an irate executive protesting, "There must be a mistake. My secretary made a reservation for me"? I don't want to sound cynical, but in the vast majority of these confrontations the disparity is due to the mendacity of the customer rather than the laxity of the restaurant.

Because maître d's worth their black ties can size a diner up better than can the legendary Belgian detective Hercule Poirot, you actually increase your chance of getting a table by being straightforward. Whenever I happen to show up at a busy establishment without a reservation, I apprise the maître d' of my plight and explain my reasons for wanting to dine at the restaurant (to enjoy the food, to celebrate a birthday, whatever). My approach has disarmed numerous maître d's, including the ones who guard the portals of the *haute cuisine* temples like Taillevent on the rue Lamennais in Paris. My method works because it's so refreshing for these professionals to see someone without reservations attempting to get in without bluffing.

"We'll eat quickly and be out by seven-thirty" is another stratagem that can tax the patience of conscientious maître d's. They know that if they acquiesce, the party with the seven-thirty reservation will invariably be kept waiting.

There is one connivance which most maître d's love to see pulled on them: table bribery. I can guarantee you that a person who tries to slip a ten- or twenty-dollar bill into the maître d's palm will not be tossed out unceremoniously by a pair of burly bouncers. Instead, the diner miraculously becomes the holder of the reservation for the next available table. Regrettably, the innocents who have legitimate reservations or who were ahead of the table buyer in the standby line receive the short end of this financial transaction.

COMPLYING WITH THE DRESS CODE

The closer you adhere to the restaurant's dress standards, the better treatment you will receive. Besides, an aura of formality is an important factor in the success formula of some restaurants.

An "open-collar" policy would probably cause the owners to lose more customers than they would gain. In our free-enterprise society, it is the prerogative of the restaurant, and not of the customer, to determine whether a coat and tie should be worn.

Some restaurants become so preoccupied with the rules they establish that they overlook appropriateness—which is a mainstay of good taste. During a recent heat wave, I saw a maître d' escort to a table a woman wearing—of all things!—a fur stole. Two minutes later, he refused to seat a woman who was very well groomed and nattily attired in a pair of pants. This spurned woman looked as though she had just stepped out of the pages of *Harper's Bazaar* and, under the circumstances, was better dressed than the fur-bedecked diner.

IDENTIFYING WHO'S WHO IN THE DINING ROOM

Anyone who cannot determine who's who in the hierarchy of an elegant restaurant is quickly labeled by the staff an outsider. I have summarized for you the attire, duties, and proper forms of address for various dining-room employees.

PROPRIETOR

Typical Attire: A business suit or dress (or chef's white outfit).

Principal Duties: Overall dining-room supervision (or cooking).

Form of Address: Unless you know the owner or the restaurant bears the proprietor's first name, use the Mr., Mrs., or Ms. honorific.

MAÎTRE D'

Typical Attire: Black tie and tuxedo.

Principal Duties: Takes your reservations, greets you on arrival, and escorts you to the table. Supervises the dining-room staff. Also known as the headwaiter.

Form of Address: First name. If it is unknown, say "maître d'."

CAPTAIN

Typical Attire: Black or white tie, white or colored dinner jacket, and black pants. Sometimes a tuxedo.

Principal Duties: Suggests entrées, takes your order, serves and prepares tableside dishes. If no sommelier, presents the wine list. Oversees about six waiters. Occasionally presents the bill.

Form of Address: First name. Or, if name is unknown, say "captain."

SOMMELIER

Typical Attire: Black outfit. Often sports a flat silver cup *(tastevin)* dangling from a long, thick silver necklace.

Principal Duties: Presents wine lists, offers suggestions, answers your oenological questions, brings and uncorks the wine, pours it and waits for your approval, and refills the glasses when necessary.

Form of Address: "Sommelier" (sohm-meh-l'yeh') or "wine steward." Use given name if it is known.

WAITER

Typical Attire: White or colored coat (usually less formal and cut shorter than the captain's) or long-sleeved waistcoat. Sometimes wears epaulets. May have linen wrapped around waist.

Principal Duties: Your primary contact. Fetches and serves the routine dishes and, possibly, beverages. Usually brings the check. Supervises the busboy.

Form of Address: "Waiter." Use given name only if it has been announced or if the two of you are acquainted.

BUSBOY

Typical Attire: Sleeveless waistcoat of no sartorial splendor. Outfit tends to be soiled with food stains (an occupational hazard).

Principal Duties: Sets table, adjusts place settings, refills water glasses, removes dirty tableware.

Form of Address: Do not speak with a busboy. Direct your requests through the waiter.

IDENTIFYING WHO'S WHO IN THE KITCHEN

The dining-room staff looks up to you if you know the kitchen hierarchy as well. In a classical French restaurant, the head cook is called the executive chef or *chef du cuisine*. Second in command is the *sous-chef* (underchef). Next in line are the *chefs de partie* (specialized cooks), such as the *chef poissonnier* (fish cook), *chef saucier* (sauce cook), *chef rôtisseur* (roast cook), and *chef pâtissier* (pastry cook). On the bottom rungs of the hierarchical ladder are the apprentice cooks and "scullery slaves."

WAITING FOR A TABLE

Even VIPs occasionally find themselves waiting for a table. There are sly reasons why management does not always immediately escort you to a table the moment you walk through the front door.

You've heard one line so often that it rings in your ears: "Sorry, you'll have to wait. Our reservations are running behind schedule tonight." You would think that professionals would realize the need to revamp their reservation systems after being constantly wrong every Friday and Saturday night year after year. Furthermore, in maître d' language a wait of "fifteen minutes" usually means "thirty minutes" or longer.

Why does management purposely overbook its reservations and then suggest that you wait at the bar? The main reason is greed. The restaurant wants to keep its high-profit bar busy.

You can bet ten martinis to one that the bartender doesn't slide the bowls of peanuts and pretzels in your direction as an act of charity. Management knows that the high salt content of these tidbits increases your thirst, which in turn encourages you to drink faster and buy more rounds. By the second drink, you've lost your willpower, so you eat even more pretzels and peanuts, which promotes more thirst and . . . It's a vicious circle that the booze pushers have devised.

Modern bar management has the art of amplifying booze consumption down to a science in other ways. Experience has taught the experts that people drink more if the music in a cocktail lounge is slow and moody rather than fast and upbeat. Consumption is greater if the decor is macho rather than sedate. The rate of drinking also increases when the lights are dim, when the distribution of the sexes is lopsided, or when there are a few heavy drinkers in the bar to serve as role models for the other patrons.

Owners want you to imbibe before dinner for yet another motive. Alcohol diminishes your inhibitions, and consequently you will probably run up a bigger tab at the dining table than if you remained completely sober. Unfortunately, boozing can also kill your taste buds.

Some restaurateurs will not seat you in the dining room until all your tablemates have arrived. This policy is justifiable only when a restaurant is very busy and you have booked, say, a table for four and two or three of your dining partners are late. However, if only one member is missing in your party of four, reason with the maître d' to seat you immediately. After all, had you originally booked reservations for three people, you probably would have been assigned a table for four anyway.

OBTAINING A GOOD TABLE

The best tables in an exclusive restaurant are normally held in reserve for regulars. They are also held in abeyance for the possible impromptu arrival of a celebrity. In the eyes of many other diners in the restaurant, luminaries decorate an establishment with as much glitter as a crystal chandelier, and their presence confers on the restaurant illustrious status. For these reasons, some restaurant owners gladly pick up the tab when a celebrity graces their establishment.

You don't necessarily have to be a regular or a celebrity to get the best or, at least, a good table. The odds are in your favor if you are, or are being accompanied by, a beautiful and well-dressed woman. Being, or being with a handsome, well-groomed man works to your advantage, too. Managers of stylish restaurants like to "dress the room."

A master practitioner of this art was Henri Soulé, whose Le Pavillon restaurant in Manhattan was the premier French restaurant in America until Soulé died in 1966. One evening when his dining room was especially aglow with distinguished gents and elegant ladies, he boasted to an associate, "Look how beautiful our Pavillon is tonight!" He would assign tables as carefully as he selected staff, menu, and food. If a party was ugly, unsophisticated, or poorly dressed, he would exile them to a location that restaurateurs call Siberia, a spot that is distant from where favorite customers sit. At times, Soulé dealt with his designated pariahs in a more insulting way: he would eclipse their faces and tacky clothes by placing in front of them on their tables a large vase of two dozen long-stemmed roses.

Nearly every restaurant has a few terrible tables. They can be near swinging kitchen doors, malodorous rest-room portals, drafty air-conditioner vents, noisy and unsightly service stations. Another inferior location is under the peering eyes of hungry diners standing in the waiting line. A cramped or postage-stamp-sized table is also unacceptable. On full nights, some people will have to sit at these undesirable tables. You should make it your business not to be one of those unfortunates, because, after all,

the prices on the menu are the same whether you sit at an unpleasant or a choice table. Your chances of getting a better table
may be better than you think because of the competition factor.
Most diners who are assigned an inferior table do not ask for a
better one. As Mark Twain said, "Let us be thankful for the fools.
But for them the rest of us could not succeed."

The first step in getting a good table, as I mentioned in the
"Telephoning for Reservations" section (pp. 26–28), is to ask for
one. Then, when you arrive, enter the restaurant with authority.
Look the maître d' square in the eye and say civilly but with as
much poise and self-confidence as you can muster, "I'm Mrs.
Marshall. I have a reservation for a table for two at nine o'clock.
You said you would reserve a nice table for me. I presume it's
ready." Remember, the meek inherit the worst tables.

Case the joint as you are waiting to be seated. Make a mental
note of the desirable spots. In fashionable restaurants, the in area
is near the entryway where you can see and be seen by all the
other diners as they enter and depart the premises. If you are
having a sub rosa meeting, a quiet table in the corner would
probably be your best bet.

Banquettes or regular tables—which are better? Socially conscious diners often prefer banquettes because, with their back to
the wall, they can scan the room, taking in the decor and people
(dining is sometimes a spectator sport). Executives generally like
the standard tables because eyeball-to-eyeball contact helps them
assess the resolve and veracity of their dining partners. Besides,
they won't risk getting a stiff neck from spending half the meal
looking sideways.

Some restaurants are multiroomed. In most cases, the best
chamber is the one nearest the maître d's stand. Overflow rooms
tend to have poorer service and ventilation and less ambiance.

If you did not request a choice table when you telephoned your
reservation, ask for a good location while you are still at the
maître d's reservation stand. Your chances of getting one increase if you arrive before or after the peak hours.

If you see that you are being escorted to an unpleasant table,
make an urbane protest before you sit down. Stand your ground
and, if appropriate, discreetly point at a table or general area that
you would prefer. Unless the table is reserved or is being kept
vacant for regulars or celebrities who might show up unex-
pectedly, you'll probably get it—even without giving the maître
d' a few dollars. One maître d' told me, "I don't mind giving

newcomers one of my best tables—or at least a better one than I assigned them to—if they ask for it. Their request tells me they're going to appreciate the difference. When I'm fully booked, you know I'm not going to waste a good table on strangers who don't make a stink when I put them over there next to the rest room."

THE HUMAN FACTOR

Many diners deny themselves VIP treatment because they overlook a basic principle: waiters are human, too. Only the most indifferent of waiters would respond unfavorably when you make an effort to be courteous and to learn their names. Only the most self-controlled waiter would not react to pretentiousness, condescension, rudeness, and unreasonable demands. As the adage goes, honey draws more flies than vinegar.

3

Ordering
the Food

Now that you are comfortably seated at the table of your choice, your next step is to order the meal. This is not as simple as it may seem. You must overcome many obstacles, including clever menu deceptions and frustrating waiters.

MENU FRAUD AND HYPE

George Bernard Shaw penned, "All professions are con-
spiracies against the laity." Menu writing is a profession.

I've come across hundreds of menu shams that have duped
unwary diners. Be on the lookout for these common misrepresen-
tations:

Aged steak is not aged, at least not the traditional way (the meat
should be hung uncovered for three to six weeks in a spacious
refrigerator with low humidity and at a temperature just above
freezing). Instead, the meat is "aged" in a vacuum plastic bag for
only a few weeks in order to reduce storage and shrinkage costs.
With this pseudo aging method, the beef is not as tender and
flavorful.

Baked on the premises refers to breads and pies that are purchased in a frozen state, then popped into the oven.

B&B one dollar is buried at the bottom of the menu in eye-
straining agate type. I've always wondered whether restaurateurs
who use the abbreviated form of the bread and butter fee have
ever heard a customer innocently say, "Fetch me a B&B liqueur—at a buck, it's quite a bargain in a fancy place like yours."

Bay scallops are sea scallops. The latter are bigger than but not
as sweet or as tender as the bay scallops.

Black Angus beef is the meat of any bovine, including a retired
dairy cow.

Buttery peas are vegetables sauced with butter diluted with
margarine. Sometimes they are sauced with margarine plain and
simple.

Champagne sauce is concocted with a run-of-the-mill domestic
Chablis.

Charcoal-grilled steak was cooked in a microwave oven rather than on a grill. The sear marks were mechanically branded on the meat at a food factory. Charcoal flavoring comes out of a spray can.

Chef's secret ingredient is rather conventional. For example, thyme in a French restaurant, oregano in an Italian restaurant, dill in a Swedish restaurant, cardamom in an Indian restaurant, five spice in a Sichuan restaurant, palm nut oil in a West African restaurant, patis in a Philippine restaurant, and lemon grass in a Vietnamese restaurant.

Chicken salad is turkey salad. And the turkey could well be pieces cut from an additive-laden processed turkey roll.

Chocolate mousse is a chocolate pudding made airy by the addition of gelatin.

Dover (or English) sole is lemon sole, summer flounder, or another less flavorful flatfish.

Famous modifies obscure dishes. One restaurant in my neighborhood had the unmitigated gall to print *Our Famous Veal Scaloppine* on its menu before its grand opening.

Fresh fruit salad contains orange and grapefruit segments that are purchased in glass bottles. The addition of a few fresh melon cubes does not justify the title "fresh fruit salad."

Fresh garden vegetables are canned or frozen. If by chance, they are fresh, they are withered and cooked hours beforehand.

Hollandaise sauce is hollandaise in name only. It is a factory-made superstabilized slop, the kind most restaurants use to top their eggs Benedict, asparagus, and broccoli. Genuine hollandaise sauce is not difficult to make once you get the hang of it. Yet few chefs bother, because it can't be made in volume and—since the emulsion breaks down easily—the sauce is a poor keeper.

Homemade soup is souped-up canned soup. Since *homemade* implies made from scratch, shouldn't the chef do much more than add a few flavoring agents and garnishes to a processed product? An even greater issue is whether a commercial kitchen should use the word *homemade* in the first place.

Idaho baked potatoes are dug out of the soil in states such as Maine and New York.

Imported is domestic. Wily menu writers frequently misuse this term because it has cachet and few diners are discriminating enough to detect the difference between the American and the foreign product.

Jambon de Bayonne in a French restaurant is an American-made prosciutto.

Lobster tails are the tails of a nonlobster species such as the sea crayfish, or the so-called spiny lobster or rock lobster of South Africa. The pseudo lobster tail virtually always arrives at the restaurant in a frozen state. The true lobster belongs to one of these species: *Homarus americanus* (New World) or *H. vulgaris* (Europe).

Long Island duckling comes from states like North Carolina.

Maple syrup is dyed corn syrup rather than the natural, boiled-down sap of the sugar maple tree.

Nova Scotia salmon is smoked salmon that has never even been close to the Maritime Provinces.

Parmesan cheese is a soapy processed cheese—perhaps even a nondairy product.

Pâté de maison comes out of a can or—if the appetizer is fresh—is bought from a purveyor. Similar misused descriptives include "our very own" and "the chef's . . ."

Peaches and cream is peaches served with half-and-half. If heavy cream is used, as it should be, the dairy item is sometimes diluted with milk or water.

Red snapper is a red porgy, gray snapper, or any one of the other relatively bland, flabby-textured fishes that bear a vague resemblance to the red snapper.

Roquefort dressing is blue cheese dressing, and, when the substitute is made, the blue cheese is of mediocre quality.

Saffron rice is given its yellow tint with turmeric, annatto seed, or food coloring rather than with the hundred-dollar-per-ounce saffron pistils. Consequently, the dish lacks the enticing flavor of saffron.

Scampi are jumbo shrimp. True scampi and prawns have miniature lobsterlike claws.

Sixteen-ounce sirloin steak weighs one or two ounces lighter than it should or includes more fat and bone than is normal.

Soufflé Grand Marnier is flavored with a cheap neutral spirit laced with orange juice.

Swordfish is some kind of shark—probably a shark of the mako species.

The authentic chili con carne recipe is an absurdity. There is no one and only culinary formula for this or virtually any other dish, be it Boston baked beans, Caesar salad, Creole chicken gumbo,

Indian pudding, Philadelphia pepperpot, or Southern fried chicken.

Three-egg omelette is made with three peewee-sized eggs which have a combined volume equivalent to about two of the eggs which most people use in their homes. When a restaurant does advertise "jumbo eggs," there's a chance that it's using pre-scrambled eggs that are shipped from a wholesaler in plastic containers.

Truffle bits are minced black olives or chopped ersatz truffles made in factories especially for the restaurant trade.

U.S. Prime beef is not U.S. Prime grade but, rather, a lower one such as U.S. Choice. "Prime ribs of beef," by the way, are not necessarily U.S. Prime ribs of beef. The epithet "prime" without the "U.S." prefix, refers to the ribs which are situated nearest to the middle of the bovine.

Virginia ham doesn't come from Virginia and is a bland, canned, 10-percent-water-added ham. Sometimes it is smoked pork shoulder or a pressed amalgam of pig's parts rather than ham at all.

Disappointment should also be expected if you place an order based on a photograph of the dish accompanying the menu. Rather than a perfect picture, your plate of shrimp might look like a visual disaster. The crustaceans will seem smaller and duller than the beauties in the photo—and there may be fewer of them, too. Moral: Don't judge a dish by its picture. My favorite example of the striking dissimilarity between the picture and the product is the oversized color photograph of a plump Big Mac that hangs over the service counter in McDonald's; it bears slight resemblance to the hamburger that is placed on your tray.

Certain posh restaurants automatically present a menu without prices to a woman when she is accompanied by a man. This policy is outright sexist. It may also make her uneasy because, if she has accepted a man's offer to pay, she may want to avoid the possible embarrassment of ordering something extravagant beyond her host's resources. The only time that a "priceless menu" should be given to a guest is when the host specifically requests this approach. If you are hosting a dinner party at a restaurant, for instance, you might find this to be a nice touch.

Be wary of menus that offer extensive selections. More often than not, the menus are more ambitious than the chef. To support a grandiose menu, a restaurant is usually forced to use a sweeping array of canned and frozen processed foods. It's been my experience that nearly all the best restaurants have limited menus.

I'm not opposed to menus written in a foreign language if the restaurant is an authentic ethnic eatery and if its target clientele understand the untranslated terms. If you don't know what *rognon de veau grillade* is, ask the waiter (or use a menu lexicon such as the French and Italian translators in Part Nine beginning on page 153).

Many restaurants, however, use foreign names on menus principally because they have snob appeal. Rather than calling the special of the day by the accurate description Roast Chicken, the restaurateur might choose Coq Claudette. (The customers, of course, don't have the slighest inkling that Claudette is the name of the chef's latest lover).

Of the various foreign languages, French has the greatest prestige in America. *Choucroute,* being French, has more mystique than *sauerkraut,* the German name for pickled cabbage. Menu writers have even tried to give pizzazz to pizza by positioning it as French Pizza.

Menu writers who stick strictly to the English language also know how to turn a phrase or two. Hamburger, for instance, becomes Prime Ground Sirloin.

Over the years, I've been collecting examples of menuese, the menu vernacular typically used in hard-sell restaurants. Good restaurants seldom use menuese—if they're serving roast duckling, they state Roast Duckling without any embellishment. Here's a brief lexicon of some of the verbal garnishes that are popular with those restaurateurs who have an inferiority complex about the down-to-earth goodness of their food:

bursting with flavor
cooked to a turn
created by our gourmet chef
crowned with
finger-lickin' good
fit for a king
from Davy Jones' locker
just for you
kettle-simmered
kissed by the sun
on a bed of
sizzling sirloin steak

steaming tureen of soup
to your liking
with choice morsels of

To remove the stigma of the word "frozen," some menu scribes say "fresh-frozen." Nonsense. Frozen food is frozen food.

Hyphenated-American restaurants create new dishes and give them names that imply they are traditional back home in the old country. Recently, I dined in a Mexican-American hole in the wall that served "Authentic Aztec Beefsteak." Anyone who knows history knows that a pre-Columbian Aztec never ate, let alone saw, a bull or a cow.

I'm not advocating that we completely restrict the creative endeavors of menu writers. Who could object if someone chose to use the less specific title "fish stew" to describe a preparation comprising a combination of ratfish, mudfish, and lizardfish? I certainly would not want to see a menu that was so graphic that it substituted "ground dead cow" for "hamburger," or "unborn chickens" for "eggs."

ORAL MENUS

Spoken menus are exasperating. The waiter comes to your table and proceeds to recite the menu in mellifluous tones, telling you a lot of extraneous details but never the prices. After several dishes are described in rapid sequence, you cannot remember what herb flavored the Costoletto di Vitello alla Valdostana, or what type of sauce was ladled over the poached (or did the waiter say grilled?) bluefish entrée.

Should you interrupt the waiter's spiel, you may have pressed the rewind button. The waiter will grudgingly start again from the beginning. To make matters worse, the din of the dining room muffles every fifth phrase.

If you hear the entire oration, you probably have been told only of those menu items the waiter could remember or was instructed to plug.

A minivariation of the spoken menu is the practice of reciting the daily specials. This is fine with me as long as the waiter mentions the cost, because some restaurants try to swell their nest eggs by shamefully overpricing their off-the-menu specials. They correctly assume that most Americans are too insecure to ask, "And what is the price of this Agneau d'Avignon?" Europeans, in contrast, are more inclined to ask a waiter a hard question which affects their pocketbooks or stomachs.

THE CREDIBILITY OF THE WAITER

The recommendation of a waiter should not be taken at face value unless you know this staffer. The waiter, following the instructions of the owner, might be pushing whatever the kitchen has in surplus. Chinese waiters often suggest bland entrées to non-Chinese diners because they don't wish to risk having the dish returned to the kitchen. Still other waiters recommend entrées based upon their at-home taste standards, which sometimes don't rise above fast-food fare and TV dinners.

Occasionally you will hear a waiter say, "Don't order that dish—it will take at least forty minutes to prepare." In many cases the dish can be made in ten to twenty minutes. The waiter attempts to steer you away from ordering these specialties, because they require too much of the chef's time and consequently are unprofitable. However, the restaurant will gladly prepare these dishes for regulars. If you want a specially prepared entrée, insist on having it.

Good waiters make the effort to learn how the dishes are prepared and take satisfaction in sharing their knowledge with their customers. These professionals, I'm sad to report, seem to be a dying breed.

Recently I asked a waiter in a Chinese restaurant how his chef prepared the stir-fried crab that was the house specialty. He responded, "The dish is too complicated for you as a Westerner to understand." When I followed up my initial query with a few more questions, I discovered the ulterior motive for the waiter's condescending attitude: he didn't know the answer, and he knew less about Shanghai cuisine than I did. Asking him anything about the food in the restaurant was about as productive as eating with greasy plastic chopsticks, so I called over the manager and received the information I sought.

Many a waiter in a French-American restaurant has evaded my "How is this sauce made?" query with contemptuous Gallic shrugs designed to imply that only an unsophisticated diner would not know the full list of ingredients for Sauce Morbouleau (which is as unknown as its village namesake in Brittany). In these cases, the waiter's uniform is indeed the last refuge of the incompetent.

The world is teeming with waiters who overestimate their gastronomic knowledge while underestimating that of the customer. I once asked a waitress, "What is the soup du jour?" She replied, "Soup of the day." I also have heard culinary lightweights smugly explain to me in agonizing detail the preparation of a simple dish.

Sometimes it is the absence of information that causes you grief. You order a side dish of vegetables because you erroneously assume they do not accompany the entrée, and the waiter remains silent. It is always a good habit to ask the waiter to specify which foods come with your entrée. This practice also gives you the opportunity to request a substitute should you dislike, for example, boiled turnips.

Waiters can also be masters of verisimilitude. I recall a French waiter in Cincinnati assuring me, "Our turbot is absolutely fresh. I guarantee you it has never been frozen." The waiter forgot to qualify his enthusiasm with the fact that the turbot was caught in European waters and flown via New York to Cincinnati, a journey that normally takes several days between hook and plate. Though he was correct in saying that the food was never frozen, he neglected to add that it was shipped partially buried in crushed ice—a preserving method that can do almost as much damage as freezing to the flavor and texture of the fish.

PLAN AHEAD

A number of situations require that you give fair warning to the waiter. If you are going to the theater or have another set engagement, tell your waiter. Most waiters will take you under their wings by expediting your order—or at least by attempting to keep your meal proceeding at a steady pace. Will you be needing a taxi? Save waiting time—instruct the waiter to call for one in advance.

Chocolate soufflés and other made-to-order specialties that take time to prepare must be requested at the beginning of the meal. Having cheese? Ask the waiter if the cheese is currently in the refrigerator. If so, ask this staffer to remove it at the onset of the meal so that the cheese will be at room temperature by the time you are ready to eat it.

Waiters make out checks for tables, not individual diners or

couples. It's up to the customer to specify "separate checks"—
and to do so before the waiter starts scribbling orders on the pad.
Some waiters try to make work easier for themselves by attempting to talk you out of your request for separate checks. Don't
yield your prerogative, because it may force you or a tablemate to
assume the role of accountant. The messy collection and redis-
tribution of funds among a group may end a meal on the wrong
note.

WHO PLACES THE ORDER

Normally, the host gives the order for the entire table to the
waiter, making sure that the staffer knows who gets which dish. If
there is no host, each adult and mature child voices his or her own
order.

WHAT NOT TO ORDER

Your goal is a well-orchestrated meal. Ideally, each dish—from
the appetizer to the dessert—should have its own distinctive
cooking style, main ingredient, seasoning, color, and texture.
You would not want to order, for example, a cream of asparagus
soup if you plan to have a veal stew enriched with cream. Neither
would it be wise to precede a delicately flavored dish with a well-
seasoned one.

A classic example of inept ordering is for a group of diners in a
Chinese restaurant to say, "We'll all have chop suey." These
gastronomic illiterates make three basic mistakes. First, chop
suey is not an authentic Chinese dish. Like the fortune cookie, it
was invented in America. Second, chop suey is monotonously
brown because, as Chinese chefs know, the average American
diner loves the sight of soy-sauce-infused food; Chinese diners
demand color contrast. Third, Chinese cuisine was never meant
to be consumed on a one-dish basis. Each of the individual dishes
tastes better if it is eaten in conjunction with others.

I recommend ordering and sharing a variety of dishes in non-
Chinese restaurants, too. This approach makes dining more exciting, and—equally important—it helps prevent sensory fatigue.
Waiters in better restaurants will usually accommodate you if you
tell them that you and your tablemate wish to share each other's

entrée. Your waiter will serve on your plate a half portion of each
entrée—or will furnish extra side plates, allowing each of you to
transfer the food. Alternatively, you can put a small portion on
your tablemate's bread or dinner plate. It is, however, considered
improper etiquette to eat directly from another's plate.

Don't assume that a One from Column A and Two from Column B menu—or a set-priced menu from any type of restaurant—
is a bargain. In most instances, it is not. On many menus I've
seen, if you ordered the same items on an à la carte basis, the
difference in cost would be negligible. Besides, by ordering à la
carte you get what you want rather than what the set menu dictates. If you don't want cream of celery soup in the first place,
why be forced to eat and pay for it?

Set menus have another drawback. Often the dishes are prepared in bulk ahead of time. À la carte selections are more likely
to be cooked to order.

Don't order for status—do it for taste. Take the pastrami sandwich. It is revered by connoisseurs, but not by the socialites
because it is relatively common and inexpensive. I know too
many people who would forgo a well-made $3.95 pastrami sand-
wich in favor of a thawed and overcooked $13.95 lamb chop out
of fear of seeming boorish to their fellow diners. Pity.

Certain menu items, such as caviar and smoked salmon, are
often the identical products which are sold in retail stores for one-
third to one-half the price in restaurants. Since you can usually
get these items at home as easily as you can order them at a
restaurant, it makes sense to try something original—uncanned
and unpackaged—when you dine out. You might as well test the
chef's culinary skill; anyone can pry open a can of pâté or pull the
cellophane off a package.

Also don't order what you can easily cook at home. Veal piccata and sole amandine, for instance, are dishes that are clearly
within the skill of most amateur cooks. Most restaurant dishes
are, in fact, easier to make than many diners suspect. The $14.50
Sole à la Veulettes might be no more than a broiled fillet that was
topped with a Parmesan-enriched white sauce and then briefly
run under the broiler. This simplicity is frequently behind a chef's
hesitance to give out his recipes: if the diners knew such "secrets," the mystique surrounding the chef's gourmet cooking
would quickly evaporate.

House specialties—unless they are the type prepared en masse
in advance—are usually your best bet when trying a new restau-

rant. Most establishments take pride in these preparations. Because many people are ordering the dish, the ingredients are probably fresh.

Contrary to popular belief, a full-scale dinner can be complete without a sweet dessert. In most parts of the world, including China and India, sweet desserts are seldom eaten with dinner. Gourmets in these areas usually end their repasts with a less heavy and less filling food, such as fresh fruit. Sweets are generally saved for special between-meal festivities—such as when a friend comes over to visit. The Western idea of finishing a dinner with a sweet, calorie-laden dessert is a relatively modern innovation—less than a few centuries old. It is also an innovation which should not be construed as law, and, except on special occasions, most of us would be better off skipping dessert.

BE ADVENTUROUS

Shying away from certain foods does not prevent a person from reaching gourmethood—virtually everyone has deep-rooted personal aversions. The "never" list of true gourmets, however, should fit on the back of a business card.

I happen to be an inveterate eclectic. I'll experiment with anything at least once, as long as it is wholesome and well prepared and not on the endangered species list. In fact, I'll bite into almost any new food, as long as it doesn't eat me first, as a lion almost did in Africa when I forgot to roll up the window of my Land-Rover.

ASK, ASK, ASK

Don't be afraid to reveal your gastronomic ignorance—this exposure is an essential element of the learning process. If more diners were to ask questions, the collective food knowledge of restaurant-goers would not be so woefully weak. According to a survey, two-thirds of the American public doesn't know the animal source of veal.

If a preparation is unfamiliar to you, ask the order taker how it is made—the dish might appeal to you. While you are at it, ask whether there are any off-the-menu specialties.

'TIS THE SEASON FOR ASPARAGUS

Never pass up the opportunity to order fruits and vegetables at the height of their seasons. They are at their best in terms of taste, appearance, nutrients, and price. Here's a peak-season calendar for some of the popular produce items:

January: broccoli, cauliflower, sweet potatoes, spinach.
February: avocados, broccoli, sweet potatoes, spinach.
March: avocados, broccoli, sweet peas, spinach.
April: artichokes, asparagus, avocados, broccoli, sweet peas, strawberries, spinach.
May: artichokes, asparagus, broccoli, papayas, sweet peas, rhubarb, strawberries.
June: beets, blackberries, blueberries, cantaloupes, cherries, corn, mangoes, raspberries, strawberries, watermelons.
July: beets, blackberries, blueberries, cantaloupes, cherries, corn, eggplants, nectarines, okra, peaches, plums, raspberries, tomatoes, watermelons.
August: beets, blackberries, corn, cantaloupes, eggplants, honeydews, nectarines, okra, peaches, plums, tomatoes, watermelons.
September: beets, cauliflower, corn, eggplants, grapes, honeydews, okra, tomatoes.
October: beets, broccoli, brussels sprouts, cauliflower, grapes, pomegranates.
November: broccoli, brussels sprouts, cauliflower, pomegranates, sweet potatoes.
December: broccoli, brussels sprouts, cauliflower, spinach, sweet potatoes.

Use these monthly lists only as rough guides, because occasionally you will discover a perfect fruit or vegetable harvested a month or two before or after its peak season. The precise season varies by region; the Sun Belt states generally enjoy the longest periods. Should any item be imported from New Zealand or another Southern Hemisphere nation, the seasons there are topsy-turvy. Some fruits and vegetables—including bananas and carrots—are available in prime condition anytime, be it Fourth of July or Christmas Eve.

"Eat oysters only during months spelled with *r*" is an anti-quated health rule. Though this advice made sense in the days before widespread refrigeration, an oyster dredged today in the hot-weather months of May through August is stored and shipped chilled. The one drawback of eating midsummer oysters is that they may be spawning and therefore would be less plump and more watery than usual.

Summer is an especially good time to cut back on high-sugar foods. Ice cream and even soda pop will make you thirsty. You become dehydrated because your stomach draws extra water from the rest of your body to help it digest the sugar. These sweeteners also make you feel hotter.

Your body demands more liquid during the scorching summer months because it loses large amounts of water through perspira-tion. Besides your intake of nonsugary beverages, think in terms of high-liquid foods such as soups, fruits, and soft-textured vege-tables.

A fatty diet can make you feel sluggish during hot weather because fat takes twice as long to digest as protein or carbohy-drates. Come winter, your need for fat increases. It helps keep you warm by fueling your body's furnace for hours on end.

THE CHILI IMMUNITY FACTOR

The ability to eat hot and spicy foods derives chiefly from an acquired immunity rather than from innate talent or mental tough-ness. The more frequently you consume chilies, the less fiery they will seem. Therefore, it would be inconsiderate for chili lovers to tell the waiter to make a dish "as hot as hell" if their tablemates who will be sharing the dish have a low tolerance level for chili peppers.

Through my years of travel in countries featuring hot and spicy cuisines, I have developed a fondness and tolerance for dishes that are well seasoned with chili peppers. When I want to eat in a Sichuan restaurant, I try to dine with people whose tolerance level more or less equates with mine. In this way, no compro-mises are needed. The food will not seem mild to me. Neither will it be palate-scorching to my dining partners.

GASTRONOMIC PYROMANIA

I'm always suspicious that people who love to see their meat entrées flambéed on the service cart are really arsonists rather than gourmets at heart. The meat is better cooked in the kitchen, where the chef has a sufficient source of high heat—these table-top burners simply don't produce the necessary heat. Also, the chef in the kitchen is more concerned about cooking your meal properly than he is about entertaining you with theatrical hocus-pocus.

GASTRONOMIC MACHOISM

Many pseudogourmets are guilty of gastronomic machoism. They order for the sake of shocking their tablemates rather than pleasing their own palates.

I recall dining with a friend who boldly announced to the waiter and everyone within earshot, "I'll have the *mogliatelle*" (Italian for sheep's testicles). I am certain that she ordered this delicacy to impress the other dinner guest, because it was I who ended up eating most of her meal. Her machoism got her the attention she desired, but it left her rather hungry.

4
Choosing
the Beverage

Wines, beer, spirits, liqueurs, and cocktails enhance the meal, especially if you know how to
order them. Part Four gives you wine pointers,
including what to do when the sommelier pours a
sample in your glass. You will also be able to
pronounce the names of almost every wine you
encounter. There are special tips on beer drinking, in addition to a handy Drinker's Lexicon on
pre- and post-dinner potables.

WINE

Spotting Poor Values: You should generally avoid the second-lowest priced wine on a list. Most restaurateurs give the greatest markup to this wine because they know that many budget-conscious diners shy away from the cheapest wine; these customers don't want to be labeled tightwads by the waiter and they suspect that the lowest-priced wine may be a bomb. Since they have neither the money nor the knowledge to choose from among the more expensive wines, these diners choose what appears to be the logical alternative: the second-lowest-priced wine.

One of the poorest values on a wine list is Pouilly-Fuissé, because of the law of supply and demand. Supply of the genuine Pouilly-Fuissé can't be expanded, because French government regulations set a limit on the number of liters that can be produced. Demand is huge, since millions of Americans routinely buy it—chiefly because they can pronounce Pouilly-Fuissé better than the names of similar-quality French wines that sell for half the price.

I occasionally see lists featuring wines from unheard-of vineyards at unheard-of prices. The wholesale cost of one wine that was being sold at twenty-five dollars a bottle was probably twenty-five dollars a case. Though most restaurateurs do not engineer such outrageous markups, they do charge from four to five times the price they pay for a bottle of wine. This is clearly too much for an item they don't have to prepare in the kitchen. In France and Italy, the average restaurant merely doubles the wholesale price.

Sometimes the restaurant sets a high price for reasons other than making a direct profit. I remember seeing a 1929 bottle from a lackluster vineyard listed on a wine card for three hundred dollars. I asked the restaurant's owner why he charged so much for it, and he replied, "The price gives my wine list a touch of grandeur, and it makes all my other wines seem less expensive by comparison. If a customer wanted to buy the bottle, I would talk him out of it. That bottle as a sales gimmick is worth more to me than three hundred dollars."

Ethnic Restaurants: The wisest choice in an ethnic restaurant is often the wine from the corresponding country. Proprietors know more about these wines than they do about the other ones they buy.

Decorative Wine Racks: If a restaurant seems to be storing a large wine supply in those eye-catching wine racks in the dining room, be on guard. Dry, warm, and well-lit environments damage wine.

Bring Your Own: When making your reservations, ask the restaurant if it has a license to sell alcoholic beverages. If not, inquire if you can bring your own (BYO). Most "dry" establishments will say yes.

Corkage: Even though a restaurant sells wine, ask if it will extend you the privilege of bringing your own bottle for a fee. This charge, usually five dollars in most restaurants, is called corkage. The advantage of paying a corkage fee is twofold. First, you save money. A bottle of wine that would cost you twenty dollars in a restaurant would normally cost only six or—at most—ten dollars in a retail wine store. You save even more because the tip and sales tax will be based on the five-dollar corkage fee rather than on the twenty dollars you would have spent if the wine was bought at the restaurant. The second benefit is selection. The retail outlet usually has a much broader choice of wines.

The Wine List: If the wine list is not handed to you by the time you receive the menu, ask that it promptly be delivered to you. To order intelligently you need to cross-consult the choice of foods and wines.

A decent wine list should offer a well-rounded selection. It should also have a few moderately priced but drinkable bottles for diners with thin wallets.

Don't automatically be impressed with a jumbo wine list—it can be just as disconcerting as a skimpy one. The most unwieldy wine list that I've seen was in a Florida restaurant. It was four inches thick, weighed five pounds, and itemized more than five thousand wines. I was afraid that the cook might go home before I had a chance to find one of the wines I was looking for. When I finally got down to ordering, the waiter kept repeating, "I'm so sorry, we've run out of that wine, too," or "We no longer have that particular vintage." This wine list could best be described as a historical record of the wines the restaurant once stocked.

Vintage Chart: Nearly as silly as following a vintage chart blindly is saying, "Vintage ratings are worthless." While many experts have no need for these tables, neophytes are advised to carry one in their wallets (many liquor stores supply them free). After all, having some data is better than having no information at all—provided you recognize that a vintage chart is not a wine bible and is perforce a generalization. A table can only give averages, and therefore, in any given region, you are bound to find some good wines produced in a bad vintage and some bad wines made during a good year.

Problems with Great Red Wines: Seldom does it make sense to order a topnotch red wine, such as classified Bordeaux (like Château Margaux) or Burgundy (like Musigny), in a restaurant. One problem is immaturity. Most wholesalers and restaurateurs hardly give these wines ample aging time because of lack of space and capital.

Even if the wine has been adequately aged, your problems are not over. Sediment-laden wines are usually inexpertly handled in restaurants. Typically, the waiter jiggles the bottle on the journey between the cellar and your table and therefore disperses the sediment into the drinkable wine (ideally, the wine should be decanted in the cellar). Once on the table, the wine in the bottle is clumsily decanted—or not even decanted at all. Great reds should normally be enjoyed at home, where you can correctly decant them.

House Wines: These can be good choices when you want only one or two glasses of wine or a moderately priced carafe. Sometimes, however, these wines may not be as dry as the waiter promised. Restaurants often stock a slightly sweet house wine but instruct their waiters to describe it as dry because most diners "think dry, drink sweet." It may also be the cheapest wine the restaurateur can afford to serve.

Another potential drawback when ordering a house wine is that you run the risk of being served from a bottle opened and re-capped the previous night, which can give the wine a sour note.

Whenever you happen to be one of the first customers of the day, be sure to inquire whether the bottle was recently opened.

Wine-Food Affinities: The topic of matching wines with foods is exceedingly complex. I know. I wrote an entire book on that subject (*The Diner's Guide to Wines,* Hawthorn). Despite the intricacies of pairing wines with foods, I would like to pass on to you a few pointers.

The first principle is not to take wine-food affinities too seriously, because a mismatch is seldom disastrous. However, a sound coupling does increase your dining pleasure, so some knowledge of wine-food coalitions is worthwhile.

Ignore this hackneyed guideline:

> Red wine with red meat,
> White wine with white meat,
> Rosé or champagne with everything.

It's simplistic. It does not take into consideration such factors as how the food is prepared. For example, a light red wine is often a better choice than a white wine for roast chicken.

Other wine-food considerations include the quality of the cooking ingredients, the type of sauce, and the fat content of the dish. Fatty preparations like roast duck are best accompanied by wines possessing a fair degree of acidity. The acid content in, for example, a young Beaujolais would help cut through the duck's fattiness.

There are time-tested affinities like Chablis with oysters, Côte de Nuits with prime roast beef, brut Champagne with caviar, and vintage Porto with Stilton.

Create your own duets, too—who knows, they may someday become traditions. Be bold in your experiments, but remember that some foods do not harmonize with wine and should be avoided or used with restraint, especially in the company of delicate wines. These discordant ingredients include anchovies, artichokes, bananas, beets, bell peppers, brussels sprouts, cabbage, chocolate, cucumbers, egg yolks, endives, garlic, grapefruits, hot spices, kale, lemons, onions, oranges, parsnips, pickles, pineapples, spinach, tomatoes, turnips, and vinegar.

The finer the wine, the more this enemies' list applies. A vinegary salad, for instance, will not violate a jug wine as much as it will a George Latour Private Reserve Cabernet Sauvignon. Should you desire a vinegar-spiked salad at the same meal you are having a subtle wine, do as the French do. Have the salad served after you have finished your main entrée.

Wineglasses: The size of the glass should be at least eight ounces so you can comfortably swirl the wine to release its bouquet. You should get a new glass for each wine that is served, because wine tastes and odors do linger.

Whenever I'm dissatisfied with the size or quality of the wineglass, I ask the sommelier or maître d' if the restaurant has better stemware. Some restaurants keep on reserve a limited supply of fine (and therefore highly breakable) wineglasses for those diners who would appreciate them.

Making Use of the Sommelier: A few wine stewards are quite knowledgeable, and it would be foolish for even a wine connoisseur not to seek their advice. Besides intimately knowing their stock, they usually have a few wines of outstanding value that are not on the wine list (these sommeliers customarily stash away special bottles for those who appreciate them).

Not all wine-order takers are well informed. When you ask some waiters about the types of wine available, they respond, "Red and white." Ask them to elaborate on their revelation and they will usually resort to another stock reply: "Chablis and Burgundy." In most instances, the wines to which they're referring are neither Chablis nor Burgundy from either a geographical or a generic standpoint.

If, by chance, these waiters have picked up some oenological knowledge, it's generally superficial. They speak of a wine like Pommard as if all Pommards were uniform in style and quality. They are unaware that two Pommards can be substantially different because of variables such as vineyard, vintage, and negotiant. Sometimes the waiters haven't even tasted the wines they recommend.

Examining the Unopened Bottle: Scrutinize the bottle for negative signs. There should be no leakage on the bottle's seal, neck, or label. Neither should there be excessive air space between the cork and the liquid. The cork should not slide down into the neck when pressed with your finger. Reject the wine if any of these unpromising indicators exist. Should the waiter insist the wine is satisfactory, accept it, but make it known that you will ask for another bottle if the wine is off.

Always read the label to verify that you have been given the wine and vintage you ordered. Other data, such as the name of the shipper and importer, are useful to the wine cognoscenti.

Breathing: The cork should be pulled anywhere from several to sixty minutes before you are ready to drink the wine. This procedure is called "letting a wine breathe."

If the wine is red, full-bodied, and fully matured, it needs to breathe for only 15 minutes, just long enough to dissipate the mustiness that it has acquired through years of storage in the bottle. A much longer breathing period would divest the wine of its ephemeral bouquet.

A fine, full-bodied red wine that is immature should be allowed to breathe for thirty to sixty minutes. The prolonged contact with fresh air helps soften the unresolved tannins, which are harsh and puckerish.

Since white, rosé, and most ordinary red wines have scant or no tannin, and since these wines have spent comparatively little time in the bottle, they need to breathe for only a few minutes. A longer period would rob them of some of their desirable freshness.

Testing the Wine: The breathing period does not have to be completed to test a wine. Your analysis must, however, be predicated on how you think the wine will taste once it has been properly aerated.

Make sure the wine is opened and poured in your presence. More than a few unscrupulous restaurants have palmed off on an unsuspecting diner a bottle of wine previously opened and rejected by another customer. Some will even resort to pouring an inexpensive jug wine into an empty bottle with a fancy label.

Modern connoisseurs do not sniff the cork (you can better detect the defects you are looking for by sniffing the wine once it's poured). You should, however, read the stamped lettering on the cork. It will verify that you have received the wine and vintage of your choice (it's easy to soak off and transfer most labels).

The sommelier should pour in the host's glass a 1½-to-2-ounce sampling. Many staffers pour much less. If so, ask for more—you need a sufficient volume of wine to swirl it properly in the glass to release the wine's aroma and bouquet. The wine sample is also poured so that the host rather than the guest gets any floating bits of cork.

This ceremonial sampling stems from centuries past. The host was served first to prove to suspecting dinner guests that the wine was not poisoned.

Evaluate the wine using the basic SST sequential steps: see, sniff, and taste. When looking at the wine, hold the glass so that the background is a white surface (a tablecloth or napkin, for instance) to check for clarity, color, and body, among other characteristics. Swirl the wine before each sniffing. When tasting, concentrate first on its initial impression and finally on its aftertaste.

Accepting or Rejecting: Give the waiter a nod if the wine is satisfactory. If it is exceptional, say so.

You can also reject the wine—provided you have a legitimate reason. Avoid thinking in absolute terms when deciding whether to accept or reject a wine. Be prepared to allow for slight imperfections—unless, of course, you are spending large sums of money.

There are, however, times when even an ordinary wine is substantially off. If the sommelier or maître d' refuses to exchange the bottle, don't let the incident ruin your meal. Dine elsewhere next time, and be sure to tell your friends to do the same.

Unfortunately for proprietors, many wines are undeservedly rejected. Some diners reject bottles merely to impress their dinner guests. Others dislike a wine because they are not familiar with its true characteristics. Still others like to claim a wine is corky, a defect which seldom occurs nowadays.

Once you accept the wine, the waiter proceeds to serve your tablemates, beginning with the person on your left, and moves around the table clockwise, filling your glass last.

The glass should not be filled more than halfway. If its capacity is greater than eight ounces, a four-ounce serving is proper.

WINE PRONUNCIATION GUIDE

It can be embarrassing to mispronounce the name of a wine when giving your order to the sommelier in an elegant restaurant. Though no one could expect a diner to pronounce accurately the names of the thousand distinct wines imported to this country, this brief wine pronunciation guide should give nonlinguists a head start. The selections will cover most of the wines you will be likely to encounter, because I've compiled them from the wine lists of several dozen leading restaurants. For the sake of space, I've eliminated well-advertised brand names such as Mateus and Ruffino.

> ## KEY TO PRONUNCIATION
> (kee too pruh-nuhn′-see’ay′-shun)
>
> ′ accent mark
>
> ’ slur mark (run the connected syllables together)

Aloxe-Corton (ah-lohss′ kohr′-tohn): Dry red or white French Burgundy wine.

Alto Adige (ahl′-toh ah′-dee-jeh): Dry white or red Italian wine.

Amarone (ah-mah-roh′-neh): Dry red Italian wine.

Anjou (ahn-zhoo′): Dry white or rosé French Loire wine.

Asti Spumante (ahs′-tee spoo-mahn′-teh): Red or white Italian sparkling wine.

Ausone, Château (oh-zohn′): Dry red French Bordeaux wine.

Barbaresco (bahr-bahr-ehs′-koh): Dry red Italian wine.

Barbera (bahr-beh′-rah): Dry red Italian wine.

Bardolino (bahr-doh-lee′-noh): Dry red Italian wine.

Barolo (bah-roh′-loh): Dry red Italian wine.

Barsac (bahr-sak′): Semisweet to sweet white French Bordeaux wine.

Bâtard-Montrachet (bah-tahr′ mohn-rasch-shay′): Dry white French Burgundy wine.

Beaujolais (boh-zhoh-lay′): Dry red, but sometimes white, French wine.

Beaune (bohn): Dry red, but sometimes white, French Burgundy wine.

Bernkasteler (behrn′-kahst’luhr): Dry to sweet white German Mosel wine; the best vineyard is Bernkasteler Doktor.

Beychevelle, Château (beysh-vehl′): Dry red French Bordeaux wine.

Blanc de Blancs (blahn′ duh blahn′): White wine made exclusively from white grapes.

Blanc de Noirs (blahn′ duh n’wahr′): White wine made exclusively from black grapes.

Bollinger (bohl-lahn-zhay′): French Champagne.

Bonnes Mares (bohn mahr′): Dry red French Burgundy wine.

Bordeaux (bohr-doh′): Red or white wine from the Bordeaux region of France.

Bourgogne (boor-goh'-n'yeh): Dry red or white wine from the French Burgundy region.

Bouscaut, Château (boo-skoh'): Dry red French Bordeaux wine.

Brouilly (brew-yee'): Dry red French Beaujolais wine.

Brunello di Montalcino (broo-nehl'-loh dee mohn-tahl-chee'-noh): Dry red Italian wine.

Cabernet Sauvignon (kah-behr-nay' soh'-vee-n'yohn): Dry red wine from various nations.

Calon-Ségur, Château (kah-lon'-say-ghur'): Dry red French Bordeaux wine.

Carbonnieux, Château (kahr-bohn-n'yuh'): Dry white and red French Bordeaux wine.

Castelli Romani (kah-stehl'-lee roh-mah'-nee): Dry white Italian wine.

Chablis (shah-blee'): Either a dry white French wine (the authentic and best version) or a dry to semi-dry white wine from other nations.

Chambertin (sham'-behr-tahn): Dry red French Burgundy wine.

Chambolle-Musigny (shahm'-bohl-moo-see-n'yee'): Dry red French Burgundy wine.

Charles Heidsieck (shahrl eyed'-sick): French champagne.

Chassagne-Montrachet (shas-sha'-n'yeh-mohn-rasch-shay'): Dry red or white French Burgundy wine.

Châteauneuf-du-Pape (sha-toh-newf'-dew-pop'): Dry red French Rhône wine.

Cheval Blanc, Château (sheh-vahl' blahn): Dry red French Bordeaux wine.

Chevalier-Montrachet (sheh-vah-lee'ay'-mohn-rasch-shay'): Dry white French Burgundy wine.

Chianti (kee'ahn'-tee): Dry red Italian wine.

Climens, Château (klee-mehns'): Sweet white French Bordeaux wine.

Clos de Bèze (kloh duh behz'): Dry red French Burgundy wine.

Clos de la Roche (kloh duh lah rohsh'): Dry red French Burgundy wine.

Clos de Tart (kloh duh tahr'): Dry red French Burgundy wine.

Clos de Vougeot (kloh duh voo-zhoh'): Dry red French Burgundy wine.

Clos Saint-Denis (kloh sahn duh-nee'): Dry red French Burgundy wine.

Corbières (kohr-beh'yehr'): Dry red, or sometimes white or rosé.

Corton (kohr-tohn'): Dry red French Burgundy wine.

Corton Charlemagne (kohr-tohn' shar-leh-mahn'): Dry white French Burgundy wine.

Cos d'Estournel, Château (koh dehs-toor-nell'): Dry red French Bordeaux wine.

Côte de Beaune (koht duh bohn'): Dry red, but sometimes white, French Burgundy wine.

Côte de Nuits (koht duh nwee'): Dry red French Burgundy wine.

Côte Rôtie (koht roh-tee'): Dry red French Rhône wine.

Côtes de Bourg (koht duh bohrg'): Dry red or white French Bordeaux wine.

Côtes de Provence (koht duh proh-vahnce'): Dry to semidry red, white, or rosé French wine.

Côtes-du-Rhône (koht-dew-rohn'): Red, but sometimes white, French wine.

Dão (doughn): Dry red, but sometimes white, Portuguese wine.

Dézaley (day-zah-lay'): Dry white Swiss wine.

Dom Pérignon (dohm pay-ree-n'yohn'): French Champagne.

Ducru-Beaucaillou, Château (dew-crew'-boh-kye-yoo'): Dry red French Bordeaux wine.

Durfort-Vivens, Château (dewr-fohr'-vee-vehns'): Dry red French Bordeaux wine.

d'Yquem, Château (dee-kehm'): Sweet white French Bordeaux wine.

Échézeaux (ay-zhay-zoh'): Dry red French Burgundy wine.

Egri Bikavér (ehg'-ree bih'-koh-vahr): Dry red Hungarian wine.

Entre-Deux-Mers (ahn'truh-duh-mehr'): Dry to semisweet white French Bordeaux wine.

Est! Est! Est! di Montefiascone (ehst' ehst' ehst' dee mohn-teh-fee'ah-skoh'-neh): Dry white Italian wine.

Figeac, Château (fee-zhack'): Dry red French Bordeaux wine.

Fixin (fees'-sahn): Dry red French Burgundy wine.

Fleurie (fluhr-ree'): Dry red French Beaujolais wine.

Frascati (frah-skah'-tee): Dry to sweet white Italian wine.

Gattinara (gaht-tee-nah'-rah): Dry red Italian wine.

Gevrey-Chambertin (zhehv-ray'-shahm'-behr-tahn): Dry red French Burgundy wine.

Gewürztraminer (geh-vehrtz'-tra-mee-nuhr): Dry white French Alsace wine. California produces its own version, which is usually slightly sweeter than the original.

Givry (zhee'-vree): Dry red or white French Burgundy wine.

Grands Échézeaux (grahn zay-zhay-zoh'): Dry red French Burgundy wine.

Graves (grahv): Dry white or red French Bordeaux wine.

Gumpoldskirchner (goom-pohldz-keerk'-nuhr): Dry to sweet white Austrian wine.

Hattenheimer (hot'-tehn-hyme-uhr): Dry to sweet white German Rheingau wine.

Haut-Brion, Château (oh-bree'-ohn): Dry red, but sometimes white, French Bordeaux wine.

Haut-Médoc (oh-may-dohk'): Dry red French Bordeaux wine.

Heidsieck Monopole (eyed'-sick moh-noh-pohl'): French Champagne.

Hermitage (air-mee-tahz'): Dry red or white French Rhône wine.

Hochheimer (hahk'-hyme-uhr): Dry to sweet white German Rheingau wine.

Johannisberger (yoh-hah'-nis-bairg-uhr): Dry to sweet white German wine.

Krug (kroog): French Champagne.

Lafite-Rothschild, Château (lah-feet'-rohth-sheeld'): Dry red French Bordeaux wine.

Lambrusco (lahm-broos'-koh): Semisweet red Italian wine.

La Mission-Haut-Brion, Château (lah mee-see'ohn'-oh-bree'-ohn): Dry red French Bordeaux wine.

Langoa-Barton, Château (lahn-goh'ah'-bahr-tohn'): Dry red French Bordeaux wine.

Languedoc (lohng'uh-dohk'): Dry red French wine.

Lanson (lahn-sohn'): French Champagne.

La Romanée (lah roh-mah-nay'): Dry red French Burgundy wine.

Lascombes, Château (lahs-kohmb'): Dry red French Bordeaux wine.

La Tâche (lah tahsch'): Dry red French Burgundy wine.

Latour, Château (lah-toor'): Dry red French Bordeaux wine.

Laurent-Perrier (loh-rahn'-puhr-ree'ay'): French Champagne.

Le Montrachet (luh mohn-rasch-shay'): Dry white French Burgundy wine.

Léoville-Barton, Château (lay-oh-veel'-bahr-tohn'): Dry red French Bordeaux wine.

Léoville-Las-Cases, Château (lay-oh-veel'-lahs-kahz'): Dry red French Bordeaux wine.

Léoville-Poyferré, Château (lay-oh-veel'-pwah-feh-ray'): Dry red French Bordeaux wine.

Liebfraumilch (leeb'-frau-milch'): Semidry to semisweet Rhine wine.

Lynch-Bages, Château (lahnsh-bahz'): Dry red French Bordeaux wine.

Mâcon (mah-kohn'): Dry white or red French Burgundy wine.

Mancha (mahn-chah'): Dry red or white Spanish wine.

Margaux (mahr-goh'): Dry red French Bordeaux wine; Château Margaux is the best of the Margaux wines.

Marqués de Riscal (mahr-kays' day reece-kahl'): Dry red, but sometimes white, Spanish Rioja wine.

Marqués de Murrieta (mahr-kays' day moo-ree-ay'-tah): Dry red, but sometimes white, Spanish Rioja wine.

Médoc (may-dohk'): Dry red French Bordeaux wine.

Mercurey (mehr-koo-reh'): Dry red or white French Burgundy wine.

Meursault (mehr-soh'): Dry white, but sometimes red, French Burgundy wine.

Moët et Chandon (moh-eht' ay shahn-dohn'): French Champagne.

Montrose, Château (mohn-rohz'): Dry red French Bordeaux wine.

Morey-Saint-Denis (mohr-reh'-sahn-duh-nee'): Dry red French Burgundy wine.

Mosel (moh'-zuhl): Dry to sweet white German wine.

Moselblümchen (moh'-zuhl-bloom'-khun): Semidry to semisweet white German wine.

Moselle (moh-zehl'): Dry to sweet white French wine.

Moulin-à-Vent (moo'-lahn-ah-vahn'): Dry red French Beaujolais wine.

Mouton-Rothschild, Château (moo-tohn'-rohth-sheeld'): Dry red French Bordeaux wine.

Mumm (muhm): French Champagne.

Muscadet (muh-skah-day'): Dry white French Loire wine.

Muscadet Sèvre et Maine (muh-skah-day' seh'vruh ay mehn'): Dry white French Loire wine.

Musigny (moo-see-n'yee'): Dry red French Burgundy wine.

Neuchâtel (nuh-shah-tehl'): Dry white Swiss wine.

Niersteiner (neer'-styne-uhr): Dry to sweet white German wine.

Nuits-Saint-Georges (n'wee-sahn-zhorsh'): Dry red French Burgundy wine.

Olivier, Château (oh-lee-vee'-ay'): Dry red, but sometimes white, French Bordeaux wine.

Oppenheimer (oh'-pehn-hyme-uhr): Dry to sweet white German wine.

Orvieto (ohr-vee-eh'-toh): Dry to semisweet white Italian wine.

Palmer, Château (pahl-mahr'): Dry red French Bordeaux wine.
Pauillac (pooh-yak'): Dry red French Bordeaux wine.
Perrier-Jouët (pehr-ree'ay'-zhoo-eht'): French Champagne.
Petrus, Château (peht-trooz'): Dry red French Bordeaux wine.
Pichon-Lalande, Château (pee-shohn'-lah-lahnd'): Dry red French Bordeaux wine.
Pichon-Longueville-Baron, Château (pee-shohn'-lohng-veel'-bah-rohn'): Dry red French Bordeaux wine.
Piesporter (peez'-pohrt-uhr): Dry to sweet white German Mosel wine.
Pinot Chardonnay (pe-noh' shar-doh-neh'): Dry white wine from various nations.
Pinot Grigio (pee'-noh gree-jee'oh'): Dry white Italian wine.
Pinot Noir (pee-noh' n'wahr'): Dry red wine from various nations.
Piper Heidsieck (pye-puhr' eyed'-sick): French Champagne.
Pol Rogers (pohl roh-zhay'): French Champagne.
Pomerol (poh-muh-rohl'): Dry red French Bordeaux wine.
Pommard (poh-mahr'): Dry red French Burgundy wine.
Pommery et Greno (pohm-muh-r'ee' ay gruh-noh'): French Champagne.
Pouilly-Fuissé (poo-yee'-fwee-say'): Dry white French Burgundy wine.
Pouilly Fumé (poo-yee' fuh-may'): Dry white French Loire wine.
Pouilly-Loché (poo-yee'-loh-shay'): Dry white French Burgundy wine.
Pouilly-Vinzelles (poo-yee'-vahn-zehl'): Dry white French Burgundy wine.
Puligny-Montrachet (poo-leen'yee' mohn-rasch-shay'): Dry white French Burgundy wine.
Rausan-Ségla, Château (roh-sahn'-say-glah'): Dry red French Bordeaux wine.
Rauzan-Gassies, Château (roh-zahn'-gahs-see'): Dry red French Bordeaux wine.
Retsina (reht-zee'-nah): Dry white Greek wine with turpentinelike flavor.
Rhine (rhyne): Dry to semisweet wines from Germany's Rhine area; the finest district is the Rheingau.
Richebourg (reesh-bohr'): Dry red French Burgundy wine.
Riesling (reece'-leeng): Dry to sweet white wine from Germany and various other nations.
Rioja (ree-oh'-hah): Dry red, but sometimes white, Spanish wine.

Roederer (roh-duh-ruhr'): French Champagne.

Romanée-Conti (roh-mah-nay'-kohn-tee'): Dry red French Burgundy wine.

Romanée Saint-Vivant (roh-mah-nay' sahn-vee-vahn'): Dry red French Burgundy wine.

Rüdesheimer (roo'-dehs-hyme-uhr): Dry to sweet white German Rheingau wine.

Rully (roo-yee'): Dry white, sometimes red, French Burgundy wine.

Saint-Émilion (sahn-tay-mee-lee'ohn'): Dry red French Bordeaux wine.

Saint-Estèphe (sahn-teh-steff'): Dry red French Bordeaux wine.

Saint-Joseph (sahn-zhoh-zeff'): Dry red French Rhône wine.

Saint-Julien (sahn-zhuh-lee'ahn'): Dry red French Bordeaux wine.

Saint Véran (sahn vay-rahn'): Dry white French Burgundy wine.

Sancerre (sahn-sehr'): Dry white French Loire wine.

Santenay (sahnt'uh-neh'): Dry red or white French Burgundy wine.

Saumur (soh-muhr'): Dry to semisweet red or white French Loire wine; sometimes sparkling.

Sauternes (soh-tehrn'): Semisweet to sweet white French Bordeaux wine.

Savigny-lès-Beaune (sah-vee-n'yee'-lay-bohn): Dry red or white French Burgundy wine.

Scharzhofberger (shartz'-hahf-behrg-uhr): Dry to sweet white German wine.

Schloss Johannisberger (shlohss' yoh-hah'-nis-bairg-uhr): Dry to sweet white German Rheingau wine.

Schloss Vollrads (shlohs' fohl'-rahdz): Dry to sweet white German Rheingau wine.

Soave (swah'-veh): Dry white Italian wine.

Spanna (spah'-nah): Dry red Italian wine.

Steinberger (styne'-behrg-uhr): Dry to sweet white German wine.

Sylvaner (sill-vahn'-uhr): Dry to semisweet white wine from Germany and from Alsace, France.

Taittinger (teht-tahn-zhay'): French Champagne.

Talbot, Château (tahl-boh'): Dry red French Bordeaux wine.

Tavel (tah-vehl'): Dry to semisweet rosé French Rhône wine.

Tokaj (toh'-kye): Sweet white Hungarian wine; also spelled Tokay.

Trebbiano (trehb-bee-ah'-noh): Dry white Italian wine.

Valdepeñas (vahl-day-pane'-yahz): Dry red or white Spanish wine.

Valpolicella (vahl-poh-lee-chehl'-lah): Dry red Italian wine.

Valtellina (vahl-tehl-lee'-nah): Dry red Italian wine.

Verdicchio (vehr-deek'-kee'oh): Dry white Italian wine, sometimes sparkling.

Vernacchia di San Gimignano (vehr-nahk-kee'ah dee sahn jee-mee-n'yah'-noh): Dry white Italian wine.

Veuve Clicquot (vuhv klee-koh'): French Champagne.

Vinho Verde (vee'-n'yoh vehr'-deh): Dry white, but sometimes red, Portuguese wine.

Vino Nobile di Montepulciano (vee'-noh noh-bee'-leh dee mohn-teh-pool-chee'ah'-noh): Dry red Italian wine.

Volnay (vohl-nay'): Dry red French Burgundy wine.

Vosne-Romanée (vohn-roh-mah-nay'): Dry red French Burgundy wine.

Vouvray (voo-vreh'): Dry to semisweet white French Loire wine.

Wehlener (vay-lehn-uhr): Dry to sweet white German Mosel wine.

Zeller Schwarze Katz (zehl'-luhr shwartz'uh' kahtz): Semidry to semisweet white German Mosel wine.

Zeltinger (zehl'-ting-uhr): Dry to sweet white German Mosel wine.

BEER

More Americans are drinking beer—especially the quality imported brands—in luxury restaurants. The English, German, Scandinavians, and many other Europeans have, of course, been doing this for centuries.

Beer is a better companion than wine to spicy foods such as fiery Sichuan or Tex-Mex specialties. For heavy foods like sausages and hearty stews, choose stouts, English-style ales, malty Bavarian-style lagers, and other strong-flavored brews. Relatively tamer preparations such as sautéed veal and Southern fried chicken are better paired with more subtle beers like lagers, pilseners, and gentle ales.

Granted, wine and not beer is the better beverage accompaniment for certain styles of cookery, including *haute cuisine*. This should not suggest, however, that beer lovers would be committing a gastronomic sin if they ordered a bottle of Kronenbourg at Paris's grandest restaurants. It is done every day.

I think it is senseless to economize on beer. Order the best the restaurant has to offer, be it imported or made in one of America's "boutique" breweries. These beers have character. The cost difference between them and those bland mass-produced American brands that flood our country is only a matter of fifty cents or so. With wine, the price differential between the cheapest and most expensive bottle can be fifty or more dollars.

When you have a choice, opt for tap beer over bottled or canned beer. If it is unpasteurized, tap beer will taste fresher and better. Canned beer is the least desirable, because over a prolonged period of time the metal alters the taste of beer.

For a more detailed discussion of beers, along with their ratings, see my book; *The Gourmet Guide to Beer* (Washington Square Press). Quality beer is a subject worthy of connoisseurship.

COCKTAILS

Ordering a drink without specifying the brand is, in most instances, like playing Russian roulette with five bullets in the chamber, because the house brand of a liquor is likely to be third-rate. One of the ways I judge a restaurant's esteem for its customers is by noting the quality of the brand it serves when a customer doesn't stipulate a label.

Just because you ordered and paid for a call brand doesn't mean you'll always get it. The table attendant could have forgotten to relay your request to the bartender, or, in clip joints, the bartender could have poured your "premium" brand out of the Old Tennis Shoe bottle.

Some bartenders are instructed by the restaurateur to water down the drinks so that profits overflow. A Bloody Mary, for instance, should be a twenty-five-proof beverage. Yet it is no secret that some of the country's most famous establishments serve Bloody Marys that border on being called Virgin Marys—they have virtually no alcohol.

In some instances the watering-down process is done before the restaurant opens. The bartender dilutes a partly filled bottle of spirits with tap water.

Even if the spirits are unadulterated, you might not be getting the volume of alcohol that you think is being poured from the bottle. Miserly restaurants use pony (1-ounce) rather than standard (1½-ounce) jiggers, which are 50 percent larger. Moreover, the quantity of spirits in any glass jigger will seem greater than it really is because refraction (the bending of light waves) creates an optical illusion. The thicker the glass, the greater the visual distortion.

Ice cubes are cheaper by volume than spirits and mixers. That's why bartenders pile ice cubes into your glass even though they know that this overkill will quickly dilute your cocktail. Another money-saving trick for restaurants is to use small cubes, which occupy more space per weight than do normal-sized ones. The newfangled round-bottomed ice cubes hog even more space.

Be cautious of bars that give their glassware the "five-and-dime-store rinse." Since a glass can carry easily transmitted germs, it should be sterilized.

DRINKER'S LEXICON

Ever wish that you could sit at a bar and know the composition or flavor of practically every apéritif, cocktail, and after-dinner drink, from absinthe to zombie? This knowledge will increase your enjoyment because it will encourage you to go beyond your old standbys.

Though this succinct compendium is reasonably comprehensive, it is by no means universal. Mixed-drink recipes vary from bar to bar.

Absinthe: Anise-flavored liqueur made with wormwood, an ingredient that was supposed to addle the mind, so the beverage was declared illegal in America. Still is.

Aguardiente: Generic Spanish word for various types of spirits. Usually clear and fiery.

Amaretto. Liqueur with almondlike flavor (derived from apricot pits).

Americano: Cocktail made with Campari and sweet vermouth.

Anisette: Anise-flavored liqueur.

Apéritif: Beverage consumed before the meal to stimulate the appetite.

Applejack: Distilled from the mash of apples. Also called apple brandy.

Apry: Apricot-flavored liqueur from France.

Aquavit (akvavit): Scandinavian spirit, usually flavored with caraway seeds. Means "water of life."

Arak: Anise-flavored liqueur from the Middle East.

Armagnac: Grape brandy from southern France.

Bahia: Coffee-flavored liqueur from Brazil.

B&B: Blend of brandy (60 percent) and Bénédictine (40 percent).

Barack Palinka: Apricot brandy from Hungary.

Bacardi Cocktail: Made with light rum, lime juice, sugar, and grenadine.

Bénédictine: Herbal liqueur from France.

Between-the-Sheets: Cocktail consisting of light rum, brandy, orange-flavored liqueur, and lemon juice.

Black Russian: Cocktail made of vodka and Kahlúa.

Black Velvet: Cocktail comprising champagne and Guinness stout.

Blended whiskey: A mixture of two or more types of whiskies (for example, blended Scotch is a mixture of malt and neutral grain spirits).

Bloody Mary: Cocktail containing vodka, tomato juice, lemon juice, Worcestershire sauce, and salt and pepper.

Bobbie Burns: Cocktail comprising Scotch, sweet vermouth, and Bénédictine. Called Robbie Burns in Scotland.

Bourbon whiskey: Distilled from a mash containing at least 51 percent corn. American.

Brandy: Any spirit distilled from the fermented mash or juice of fruit, be it grapes, cherries, whatever. The unmodified name *brandy* implies grape brandy.

Brandy Alexander: Cocktail made with brandy, crème de cacao, and cream.

Brave Bull: Cocktail containing tequila and Kahlúa.

Bronx: Cocktail made with gin, dry vermouth, sweet vermouth, and orange juice.

Bull Shot: Cocktail comprising vodka, beef bouillon, lemon, and celery salt.

Byrrh: Aromatized fortified wine from France.

Café Brûlot: Cocktail made with flaming brandy, sugar, spices, orange, lemon peel, and hot coffee.

Café Royale: Cocktail made with flaming brandy, sugar, and hot coffee.

Calvados: Apple brandy from Normandy, France.

Campari: Apéritif with a bitter flavor, often mixed with soda.

Canadian whiskey: Blended spirits distilled from the mash of corn, rye, wheat, and barley malt.

Chamborg: Berry-flavored liqueur from France.

Champagne Cocktail: Comprises champagne, sugar, and bitters. Garnished with lemon twist.

Chartreuse: Herbal liqueur from France. The green-hued variety is drier and stronger than the yellow one.

Cheri-Suisse: Chocolate-cherry-flavored liqueur.

Choclair: Chocolate-coconut-flavored liqueur.

Cider: Two basic types: hard cider (fermented apple juice) and sweet cider (nonalcoholic).

Cocktail: Nowadays, a mixed drink whether served in a short or a tall glass.

Cognac: Grape brandy made in the Cognac region of France. V.S. on the label means the cognac was aged for at least three years and V.S.O.P. for at least four years in a wooden barrel.

Cointreau: Orange-flavored liqueur.

Cordial: In the United States, this term is synonymous with *liqueur* (see).

Corn whiskey: Distilled from a mash containing at least 80 percent corn. American.

Crème: Appellation given to various liqueurs.

Crème d'Ananas: Pineapple-flavored liqueur.

Crème de Cacao: Liqueur flavored with cocoa and vanilla beans.

Crème de Cassis: Black currant-flavored liqueur.

Crème de Fraise: Strawberry-flavored liqueur.

Crème de Menthe: Mint-flavored liqueur.

Crème Yvette: Violet- and vanilla-flavored liqueur.

Cuarenta y Tres: Herbal liqueur (forty-three flavoring agents) from Spain.

Cuba Libre: Rum and cola with a lime slice or segment.

Curaçao: Orange-flavored liqueur.

Cynar: Artichoke-flavored apéritif.

Daiquiri: Composed of light rum, lime juice, and sugar. A frozen daiquiri is made with shaved ice.

Danziger Goldwasser: Herbal liqueur with edible gold flakes.

Drambuie: Scotch-based liqueur flavored with honey.

Dubonnet: Deep red, slightly sweet, quinine-accented apéritif. The pale straw version is drier.

Eau de vie: Spirits in general. More specifically, a colorless spirit or fruit brandy. Literally, "water of life."

Eggnog: Punch made up of brandy, milk, egg, sugar, and nutmeg.

Forbidden Fruit: Liqueur flavored with fruits, including the grapefruitlike shaddock.

Frais: Strawberry brandy.
Framboise: Raspberry brandy.
Frangelico: Hazelnut-flavored liqueur from Italy.
Frappé: Liqueur mixed with shaved ice. Drunk with a straw.
Galliano: Herbal liqueur from Italy.
Genever: A Dutch gin.
Gibson: Substitute a cocktail onion for the olive or lemon peel in a *martini* (see).
Gimlet: Cocktail made with gin and Rose's Lime Juice. Can also be made with vodka.
Gin: Juniper-berry-flavored neutral spirit.
Gin and Tonic: Cocktail containing gin, tonic water, and lime slice or segment. Can also be made with vodka.
Gin Fizz: Cocktail made with gin, sugar, lemon juice, and soda water.
Gin Rickey: Cocktail made with gin, lime juice, grenadine, and soda water. Garnish with lime slice or segment.
Glögg: Scandinavian heated punch containing red wine, brandy, dry sherry or Madeira, bitters, and either allspice or cinnamon, cloves, and nutmeg.
Grand Marnier: Orange-flavored liqueur from France.
Grappa: Brandy distilled from the residue (skin, seeds, pulp) of pressed grapes.
Grasshopper: Cocktail containing green crème de menthe, white crème de cacao, and cream.
Grog: Dark rum or other spirit diluted with cold water. Also, dark rum mixed with lemon juice, sugar, and boiling water.
Hair of the dog: Scotch or other whiskey combined with cream and honey or sugar. A supposed morning-after remedy.
Harvey Wallbanger: Cocktail made with vodka, Galliano, and orange juice.
Herbal liqueur: Infused with a wide variety of herbs and other flavoring agents. No one flavor dominates.
Highball: Whiskey or other spirit combined with a sparkling mixer such as soda water. Served in a tall glass.
Hot buttered rum: Concoction of dark rum, sugar, nutmeg, cinnamon, cloves, and butter.
Hot Toddy: A cold-weather pick-me-up comprising whiskey, sugar, spices, and boiling water.
Irish Coffee: Mixture of Irish whiskey, sugar, and hot coffee. Topped with whipped cream.

Irish Cream: A "high-octane milk shake" product made with Irish whiskey.

Irish Mist: Irish whiskey-based liqueur flavored with honey.

Irish whiskey: Like Scotch, distilled barley mash. Unlike Scotch, not flavored with peat smoke.

Izarra: Brandy-based liqueur from the Pyrénées.

Jägermeister. Herbal liqueur from Germany.

Kahlúa: Coffee-flavored liqueur from Mexico.

Kir: Apéritif made with dry white Burgundy wine and crème de cassis.

Kirsch/Kirschwasser: Cherry brandy from Switzerland, Germany, or France.

Kümmel: Caraway- and cumin-flavored liqueur.

Lillet: Slightly sweet quinine-flavored apéritif from France.

Liqueur: Spirit that has been sweetened and flavored with aromatics.

Liquor: See *spirit*.

Lochan Ora: Scotch-based liqueur.

Madeira: Fortified wine from Madeira. Sercial and Rainwater are dry versions. Bual and Malmsey are sweet.

Mai Tai: Tropical drink made with light and dark rums, orange-flavored liqueur, lime and other fruit juices, grenadine, sugar, and Orgeat syrup. Garnished with cherries, pineapples, and mint sprigs.

Mandarine: Tangerine-flavored liqueur.

Manhattan: Cocktail made with Bourbon (or other whiskey), bitters, and sweet vermouth. Substitute dry vermouth for a dry Manhattan. Garnish with cherry if sweet or lemon twist if dry.

Maraschino: Cherry-flavored liqueur from the Dalmatian coast.

Marc: Brandy made with the leftover seeds, skins, and pulp of pressed grapes.

Margarita: Cocktail made with tequila, lime juice, and triple sec or another orange-flavored liqueur. Glass is rimmed with salt.

Marrōn: Chestnut-flavored liqueur.

Marsala: Sweet fortified wine from Sicily.

Martini: Gin or vodka plus dry vermouth. Garnished with olive or lemon peel.

Mead: Fermented honey beverage.

Metaxa: Brand name for various Greek products including brandy and Ouzo.

Mezcal: Tequilalike spirit from Mexico. Some bottles contain a whole agave worm.

Mimosa: Cocktail containing champagne, Grand Marnier, and orange juice.

Mint Julep: Bourbon and sugar mixed in shaved ice. Garnished with mint sprigs.

Mirabelle: Plum brandy from France.

Moscow Mule. Cocktail comprising vodka, lime juice, and ginger beer.

Mulled wine: Heated punch containing red wine, brandy, sherry or Porto, lemon sections, sugar, cinammon, cloves, and nutmeg.

Negroni: Cocktail made with gin, sweet vermouth, and Campari.

Nocello: Walnut-flavored liqueur from Italy.

Old Fashioned: Cocktail comprising Bourbon or rye whiskey, sugar, and bitters.

Ouzo: Anise-flavored apéritif/liqueur made from grapes, raisins, dates, figs, or sugarcane, among other possibilities.

Pasha: Coffee-flavored liqueur from Turkey.

Pastis: Anise-flavored apéritif/liqueur from southern France.

Pernod: Anise-flavored apéritif/liqueur from France.

Pidang Ambon: Dutch liqueur with Indonesian tropical fruit accent.

Pimm's Cup: One of several gin-based mixes. Often combined with ginger ale or lemonade.

Piña Colada: Light rum, coconut cream, and crushed pineapple or other tropical fruit.

Pineau des Charantes: Cognac-based apéritif from France.

Pink Lady: Cocktail made with gin, applejack, lemon juice, grenadine, and egg white.

Pisco: Grape brandy from Peru.

Pistàshà: Pistachio-flavored liqueur.

Planter's Punch: Traditional recipe: one sour (lime juice), two sweet (sugar), three strong (rum), and four weak (ice). Garnished with tropical fruits and mint sprig.

Poire Williams: Pear brandy from France.

Porto: The proper name for authentic Portuguese port. Vintage and Old Tawny are the driest, Ruby the sweetest Portos.

Pousse-café: Rainbowlike drink composed of individual layers of liqueurs of varying colors and densities.

Prairie Oyster: Brandy, vinegar, Worcestershire sauce, and ground red pepper. Garnished with raw egg yolk.

Quetsch: Colorless brandy made from a purple plum.

Raki: Anise-flavored apéritif/liqueur from the Near East. Literally, "lion's milk."

Ricard: Anise-flavored apéritif/liqueur from France.

Rob Roy: Same as a Manhattan, but Scotch is substituted for the bourbon or rye.

Rum: Spirit distilled from the mash of sugarcane or a sugarcane product (molasses, for example).

Rum and Coca-Cola: Another name for *Cuba Libre* (see). Best made with dark rum.

Rusty Nail: Cocktail containing Scotch and Drambuie.

Rye whiskey: Distilled from a mash containing at least 51 percent rye grain. American.

Sabra: Chocolate-orange-flavored liqueur from Israel.

St. Raphaël: Sweet, quinine-flavored apéritif.

Sake: So-called rice wine from Japan, served warm and drunk from tiny porcelain cups. Technically, this crystal-clear beverage is more of a beer, since it is brewed.

Saketini: Substitute sake for the vermouth, and cucumber slice for the olive or lemon peel, in a *martini* (see).

Salty Dog: Cocktail made with gin, grapefruit juice, and salt.

Sambuca: Liqueur accented with the licoricelike flavor of the elder bush. Sambuca *con mosche* is garnished with three coffee beans.

Sangría: Punch made with wine, brandy, various cut fruits, sugar, and soda water.

Sangrita: Cocktail made of tequila, tomato juice, grenadine, citrus juice, salt, and Tabasco.

Sazerac: Cocktail containing bourbon, Pernod, or Ricard, sugar, and bitters. Garnished with fruit.

Scarlett O'Hara: Cocktail concocted with Southern Comfort, orange juice and grenadine.

Schnapps: German and Dutch term for any of several flavored colorless spirits. Similar to *aquavit* (see).

Scorpion: Tropical drink comprising rum, brandy, lemon juice, orange juice, and Orgeat syrup. Garnished with a gardenia.

Scotch whisky: Distilled from barley mash and flavored with peat smoke.

Scotch Mist: Scotch poured over shaved ice. Garnished with a lemon peel.

Screwdriver: Cocktail containing vodka and orange juice.

Sherry: Fortified wine from Spain. Fino and Amontillado are among the driest types. Oloroso (in this country) and cream sherries are sweet.

Sidecar: Cocktail consisting of brandy, orange-flavored liqueur, and lemon juice.

Singapore Sling: My bartender at Singapore's Raffles Hotel (where the drink originated) used these ingredients: gin, Peter Heering, Bénédictine, Cointreau, bitters, and juice from oranges, limes, and pineapples. Garnished with fruit and mint sprigs.

Slivovitz: Plum brandy from the Balkans. Called *tuica* in Romania.

Sloe Gin: Liqueur (not a gin) flavored with sloe berries.

Sour mash whiskey: Distilled with grain mash soured with a lactic culture.

Southern Comfort: Sweet, peach-flavored bourbon.

Spirit: A distilled alcoholic beverage (distinguished from beer and wine which are, respectively, brewed and vinted but not distilled).

Spritzer: Blend of white wine and soda water.

Stinger: Cocktail comprising brandy and white crème de menthe.

Straight whiskey: Bottle contains one specific type of whiskey. Distinguished from *blended whiskey* (see).

Strega: Herbal liqueur from Italy. Literally, "witch" in Italian.

Swizzle: Cocktail comprising a spirit such as rum or gin, lime juice, sugar, and soda water.

Tennessee whiskey: Similar to bourbon, but seeped through maple charcoal.

Tequila: Colorless spirit made from the heart of the agave plant in Mexico.

Tequila Sunrise: Cocktail comprised of tequila, grenadine, and orange juice.

Tia Maria: Coffee-flavored liqueur from Jamaica.

Tom Collins: Cocktail containing gin, lemon juice, sugar, and soda water. Garnished with cherry and slice of citrus fruit.

Tom and Jerry: Hot drink comprising dark rum, egg white and yolk, sugar, nutmeg, and boiling water.

Triple Sec: Orange-flavored liqueur.

Van der Hum: Tangerine-flavored liqueur from South Africa.

Vandermint: Chocolate-mint-flavored liqueur from Holland.

Vermouth: Aromatic fortified wine. White is dry, red is sweet.

Vodka: Charcoal-filtered neutral spirit.

Whiskey: Neutral grain spirit matured in wood, which gives the beverage its brownish hue. (Spelling note: use *whiskey* for American and Irish products. In most other cases, including Scotch, use *whisky*).

Whiskey Sour: Cocktail made with whiskey, lemon juice, sugar, and either egg white or a splash of soda water.

Zombie: Tropical drink made with rum, fruit liqueurs, fruit brandies, and fruit juices. Garnished with cut fruit and mint sprigs.

NONALCOHOLIC BEVERAGES

You should refuse a defective nonalcoholic beverage as quickly as you would an off bottle of wine.

Coffee: This beverage becomes bitter or acrid if its beans are too finely ground, if the coffee was percolated (the drip method is better), or if the coffee was brewed in advance and kept on a warming plate for more than ten minutes. Harsh-tasting coffee can be the result of low-grade beans. If ground coffee beans are exposed too long to air, they will lose much of their essential oils—when brewed, the coffee will taste flat and lack a rich in-cup aroma. Coffee is also unsatisfactory if it is lukewarm, weak, or too strong. If your cream curdles in the cup, the dairy product was not fresh.

Tea: Brews made with loose tea have a fresher, more ethereal flavor than those prepared from a tea bag. Why, then, do multistar restaurants force their customers to end a superb meal with a beverage made from tea bags? At $1.50 a pot, couldn't the restaurant afford to brew fresh tea? If the establishment insists on using tea bags, the least it can do is use a quality brand. Tea also suffers from being too weak, overbrewed, bitter, or stale.

Soft Drinks: Colas and other soft drinks are too sweet for virtually all foods. Less cloying—and more healthful—are milk and fresh fruit juices. The most neglected of all table beverages is water.

Water: If your table water smacks of freezer odor, it was probably made with ice cubes that vacationed in the deep freezer. (Restaurants with this problem should rinse the cubes under cold tap water. This remedy works because freezer odor rarely penetrates the cube's surface.) It is becoming fashionable in America to order mineral water in restaurants as Europeans do. This practice makes sense in Europe because most of the local water supplies have off flavors and colors. However, in areas like New York City where the local water supply is excellent, there is less rationale for this custom.

5

Eating the Meal

Knowing the basic rules of table etiquette is crucial for any discriminating diner. So is the ability to establish rapport and lodge complaints with the staff. You will gain better service because the staff will take you more seriously.

TABLE ETIQUETTE

My earliest breach of table etiquette that I can recall occurred when I was a child eating in a ritzy Santa Barbara, California, restaurant. Much to the chagrin of my parents, I drank the water in my finger bowl. Since then, I have made countless other and equally embarrassing faux pas in gourmet temples and roadside diners alike but gradually learned the basic rules.

Some contemporary Americans disregard etiquette, believing formal manners to be too rigid and cumbersome for the modern casual lifestyle. In most instances this attitude is valid. Still, there are certain manners that are basic courtesies.

There are also times when it's good business to know the panoply of table etiquette. Consider the hapless souls who, when dining with their bosses or clients at an elegant restaurant, fidget in their chairs because they are not certain which of the two forks to use for their sole véronique. If they knew the rules of the table game, they would be more poised and self-assured, qualities that are essential to an executive.

Affected or dated manners are equally self-defeating. You know how silly and prissy people look when they daintily pat their lips after every second bite.

My selected guidelines reflect a consensus of sophisticated contemporary diners. However, no etiquette rule is engraved in stone—even Amy Vanderbilt, Emily Post, Judith Martin, and other leading authorities on manners often disagree.

The best overall advice is to heed your instincts. You are less likely to commit a gaffe if you act naturally.

SERVING:

• The waiter serves food from your left and beverages from your right side.

- When the waiter offers you a platter, help yourself with the serving fork in your left hand and the serving spoon in your right.
- Foods and beverages are passed around the table clockwise.

CUTLERY:

- Most Americans use the zigzag eating method. They cut their food with their fork in the left hand and their knife in the right. To eat the severed portion, they put down their knife and pass the fork from the left hand, through a half twist, to their right. The right hand then conveys the fork to the mouth.
- For good reason, a growing number of Americans are adopting the Continental eating style, which I prefer. With this method, the fork remains continually in the left hand (tines down) and the knife in the right. Since this technique involves no switching of utensils from hand to hand, it is more efficient and less awkward than the zigzag way. It becomes undignified, however, when the diner loads the back of the fork with a mixture of foods.
- The standard table knife is held with the butt ensconced in your palm. Your forefinger extends along the utensil's backbone to provide leverage. A fish knife is held like a pencil and is used for tearing and pushing more than for cutting.
- Finish eating a piece of meat before cutting off the next bite-sized portion.
- Most dessert dishes are eaten with a spoon. However, you eat certain dishes like crêpes Suzette and other small dessert pancakes with both fork and spoon. Only a few desserts, such as firm pies or cakes, are eaten solely with a fork.
- Leading Italian etiquette books flatly state that you should never use a spoon to help you twirl spaghetti around the tines of a fork. The proper method is to twirl the pasta around the tines against the surface of the plate or bowl.
- Because a cheese fondue pot is communal, your lips should not touch the prongs of your fondue fork when you're eating directly from the utensil.
- Don't hold a utensil when taking a drink or wiping your mouth.
- You should not let your utensil rest part on the plate and part on the table. Have the handles but never the points of your implements overhang the edge of your plate.

• The position of the knife and fork on your plate sends messages to the waiter. If your knife and fork are crossed with the curve of the tines covering the knife blade (as illustrated below), it tells a knowledgeable waiter that you are resting between bites. If you are finished, place the knife and fork parallel to each other on your plate (as depicted on page 86). The fork tines should be down and the cutting edge of the knife should face the fork. In continental Europe, please note, different systems are used.

THE REST POSITION

THE FINISHED POSITION

FINGER FOOD:

- You can eat foods like artichoke leaves, asparagus, canapés, cherries, cherry tomatoes, corn on the cob, crisp bacon, french fries, frog's legs, grapes, pizza, sandwiches, spare ribs, and strawberries with your fingers. There are exceptions, of course, such as asparagus covered with a sauce.
- With the exception of formal meals, you can use your fingers to eat the legs and wings (not the breast) of small game birds such as squabs and Cornish hens. If the poultry is very small (a baby quail, for instance), lift the whole cooked bird to your mouth with your fingers and proceed to nibble away. And there's only one sane way to eat "finger-lickin' good" Southern fried chicken.
- Occasionally, near or at the end of your meal, you are presented with a finger bowl to wash your fingertips. Should the waiter bring you one of these vessels set on a plate along with a doily,

spoon, and fork, transfer the bowl and doily to a spot slightly beyond the upper left-hand side of your plate. Then move the dessert silverware, placing the fork to the left and the spoon to right of your plate. When you are through with the entrée, dip your fingertips into the bowl and pat them dry with your napkin.

- You can suck the juice and meat out of the small legs and claws of crabs and lobsters. This is sometimes the only way to reap this succulent treasure.
- Butterfly shrimp can be dipped into a sauce and eaten with your fingers.
- If the shrimp cocktail contains shelled jumbo-sized crustaceans, pierce them near their tail with the accompanying small fork and eat the edible flesh one bite at a time.
- Indian, Thai, and certain other ethnic foods are traditionally eaten with your fingers, though you won't be out of place if you ask for silverware.

SOUP:

- When eating soup, fill the spoon by moving your utensil away from you. In America, the last drops of soup are gathered by tilting the bowl away from you.
- If consommé is served in a cup with twin handles, you may lift the cup and drink it as you would a beverage. In a Japanese restaurant, you lift the small lacquered soup bowl, even though it has no handles.

BREAD:

- Break bread by hand, not with a knife. Break it and butter it over the bread plate, and not over the dinner plate as many people do. Butter one bite-sized portion at a time.
- The sauce on a plate may be soaked up and eaten with a piece of bread that is handheld or pierced with a fork (exception: formal dining situations). The sopping custom, which compliments the chef, is popular in Europe and is catching on in America.

NAPKIN:

- Lobster bibs are tacky; so are napkins hung around the neck.
- Unfold your full-sized dinner napkin halfway before placing it

on your lap. A smaller (luncheon) napkin is unfolded completely.

- When you are ready to leave your seat, fold your napkin and place it on the table, to the left of the plate.

OTHER BASIC RULES OF ETIQUETTE:

- Do not salt and pepper foods before tasting them. To do so is to insult the chef.
- To keep from squirting your dinner companion in the eye when squeezing a lemon wedge, follow this method. First, impale the pulp of the lemon wedge on the fork tines. Next, cup your free hand over the lemon and gently squeeze the fruit.
- When served a half duck or chicken, use your knife and fork to cut the wing and leg away from the breast before you start eating any of the meat. This makes the eating process simpler and neater.
- To remove from your mouth an unwanted substance like a seed or bone bit, you have three options. Some authorities advise that the object should exit as it entered (if it comes in on a fork, it should be spit out on a fork). Other etiquette experts suggest that for morsels like gristle, it is best to put a napkin over your mouth and to spit the entity discreetly into it. Yet other etiquette authorities recommend that you spit the piece out in your cupped hand. Select the method you feel most comfortable with.
- Wineglasses are held by the stem, not the bowl.
- If you are counting calories, do not make an issue of it. Otherwise, you might make the other diners feel guilty if they are contemplating ordering, for example, a chocolate mousse for dessert.
- Go easy on perfumes and colognes. They can prevent nearby diners from fully appreciating their meal because these fragrances partially desensitize olfactory organs.
- Do not smoke until the food portion of the meal is finished, and even then ask permission from your fellow diners. Double-check to make sure that your smoke is not wafting to the next table.
- The rule that says you should always leave some food on the plate is foolishly wasteful. If you are hungry enough to finish everything, by all means do so.

- Contrary to popular belief, it is all right to put your elbows on the table once everyone has finished eating.
- My favorite etiquette rule is "Never use a matchbook to pick your teeth at a dinner table." I suppose violators risk suffering the embarrassment of having the name of some pizza joint imprinted on their incisors.

IDENTIFYING SILVERWARE AND GLASSWARE

It is easy to become socially embarrassed when you cannot identify the individual functions of all the pieces of silverware set before you at a formal dinner. The same is true for glassware.

Can you, for example, tell the difference between a fish knife and a butter knife? (The fish knife has a pointed rather than a rounded tip. It also has a tiny notch on the dull edge of its blade.) Can you distinguish a fish fork from a salad fork? (The fish fork has small notches between the bases of the tines.)

The illustrations "Identifying Silverware" on page 91 and "Indentifying Glassware" on page 90 will help you recognize the various types of knives, forks, spoons, and glasses.

Should you ever question which silverware to use when you are faced with a selection at your place setting, begin with the outermost utensil and move toward your plate in successive courses. (If the host chooses to set the silver by size, this system may not work.) The illustration on page 92 depicts a typical semiformal dinner setting.

ESTABLISHING RAPPORT AND YOUR CREDENTIALS

One of your first goals is to develop a rapport with your waiter. Try to learn his or her name. Above all, memorize your waiter's face (I frequently see diners frantically flagging the wrong waiter).

Earn the waiter's respect. Be cordial but not too familiar. Speak with authority—ask your questions and give your order in a self-assured tone.

Demonstrate your dining savoir-faire by instructing the waiter to remove any items from the table that do not belong there. In a Chinese restaurant, for instance, tell the waiter to take away the

Bordeaux   Burgundy   Taste Vin   Rhine

Flute   Tulip   Coupe*   Pilsner   Highball

CHAMPAGNE

Tumbler   Cocktail   Sherry   Cordial   Brandy Snifter

not recommended

IDENTIFYING GLASSWARE

dinner knife

luncheon knife

steak knife

fish knife

dessert knife

fruit knife

butter spreader, flat

dinner fork

fish fork

salad fork

dessert fork

cocktail fork

fruit fork

olive fork

lemon fork

iced tea spoon

soup spoon

dessert spoon

cream soup spoon

teaspoon

grapefruit spoon

afternoon teaspoon

demitasse spoon

IDENTIFYING SILVERWARE

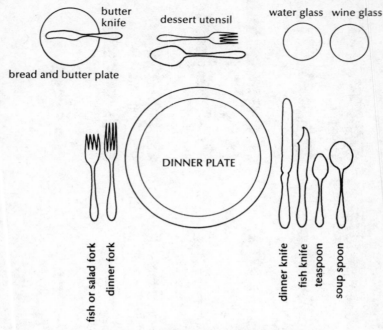

A TYPICAL SEMI-FORMAL DINNER SETTING

small bowls of mustard and duck sauce, which are unauthentic accommodations for the Westerner. Silverware should be replaced with chopsticks, if you can use them. Superfluous items should be removed, too. Extra place settings and, if no one smokes, ashtrays have no place on a properly set table.

PET PEEVES

Ever order a medium-rare steak that arrives bloody rare, and you ask the waiter to take it back to the kitchen for further cooking? Twenty minutes later, in the tradition of Freudian reaction formation, your steak returns—charred beyond recognition. When you refuse the dish and request medium-rare meat, the waiter gives you a look which clearly questions your sanity.

I'm sure you have a number of other restaurant peeves. Perhaps these are some of them:

- The waiter tries to give you the impression that you are fortunate and privileged to be dining in the restaurant.
- The waiter has not taken the trouble to learn how the daily specials are prepared.
- The menu is torn, greasy, and stained—or lacks the insert announcing the specials of the day.
- Staffers' uniforms are soiled, wrinkled, or threadbare. Hair is disheveled and untrimmed. Fingernails need cleaning and clipping. Shoes are scuffed and unpolished.
- The French waiter tries to get the upper hand by pretending he or she doesn't understand your pronunciation of *rognon de veau*. If you had originally asked for veal kidneys, the waiter would have haughtily said, "You mean the *rognon de veau,* monsieur?"
- The waiter has a marvelous sense of timing—the staffer is never in sight when you need service. Never, that is, unless the waiter is in the corner chatting with another waiter. "How many waiters do you suppose actually work in this restaurant?" I once asked my dinnermate. "About half," came her hungry reply.
- The martini and steak always seem to end up in front of the man, the vermouth and seafood salad in front of the woman. Sexism frequently surfaces in a restaurant.
- The waiter absentmindedly gives you your dining partner's order. Proficient waiters don't have to ask, "Who gets the Costoletta alla Milanese?" If a waiter can't memorize who gets what, the information should be noted on the pad.
- The waiter did not tell you the two-dollar side order of vegetables you requested automatically comes with the main entrée. Or the opposite occurs. Your fillet of sole sits by its lonesome self because you did not know the vegetables had to be ordered à la carte.
- The waiter reaches over your shoulder to serve or remove dishes from the table.
- The waiter doesn't know how to pour a bottle of wine, so the liquid dribbles onto the tablecloth and possibly onto your clothes. (When a butterfingered waiter spilled coffee on Dorothy Parker's designer gown, the great wit allegedly quipped, "Go and never darken my Dior again.")
- The waiter sets before you a cup swimming in a saucer full of coffee. This messy setting should be replaced without having to ask.
- You are served a white wine that was stored in the refrigerator

for hours if not weeks. The wine is so cold that it numbs your taste buds, preventing you from appreciating its nuances. Quality beers are served too cold, too.

- The white wine is stored in the ice bucket for the duration of the meal. Once again, the beverage becomes too cold.
- The staff is intrusive. They loiter within earshot of your intimate conversation and incessantly refill water goblets, empty ashtrays, and ask, "Is everything all right?"
- The waiter thinks that everything she or he has to say is urgent enough to interrupt your conversation with your tablemate in midsentence.
- The restaurant forces you to dine at its and not your preferred pace. The more expensive the restaurant, the less you should tolerate this practice.
- Your plate is whisked away before your companion has finished eating. This pressures the slower diner into eating faster.
- The waiter stands glowering with poised pencil while you examine the list of desserts.
- The lighting is so dim that you can hardly see your attractive date across the table or, as the management might be intending, the vulcanized vulture on your plate.
- The busboy dumps the dirty silverware and plates into the bin under the service table, creating unnerving clang and clatter.
- The piped-in music is distracting. Its poor audio fidelity creates more sound than music. Sometimes the volume is too high or too low, depending on where you are sitting, and the programmer's musical taste is questionable.
- The rest rooms are rank and untidy and need supplies.
- The ventilation is poor, and if there is an air conditioner, it's set uncomfortably high.
- The strolling violinist or accordionist obligingly plays all requests, which results in boring repetition. It's amazing how many people ask for "La Paloma" in a Mexican restaurant, "La Vie en Rose" in a French bistro, and "O Solo Mio" in an Italian hideaway.

LODGING COMPLAINTS

According to a human-behavior research study conducted by a New York University professor, four out of five patrons do not complain (either by voicing a complaint or by withholding the tip) when they receive obvious bad service or food. Their complacent motto is "Let's not make a scene, dear."

Customers should deliver their protests—if you are paying the piper, you have the right to call the tune. Besides, if you complain, you might just improve the situation for future diners. One restaurateur told me, "I prefer my patrons to make their dissatisfaction known. By protesting, they help me keep my kitchen and service staff on their toes."

One of the keys to successful complaining is to avoid getting hot under the collar. Wars of angry words and looks between a waiter and a customer have a way of escalating. Moreover, an altercation spoils the mood of your dinner, and the stress it causes can literally trigger a gut reaction. To lodge a complaint effectively, speak in a firm, composed voice.

If your waiter is unresponsive to your complaint, call for the maître d' or the owner. They have the power to reprimand an intransigent waiter. If the problem concerns food quality, they have more clout than the waiter to convince a stubborn chef that he should prepare the dish to your liking.

As with a bottle of wine, you can reject a dish if you have a bona fide reason. Regrettably, some diners send a perfectly good dish back to the kitchen simply because it tastes or looks different from the version they are accustomed to.

One problem with returning a dish is that it throws the meal out of sync. Your tablemates will be eating their food while you sit empty-handed. If your spurned dish takes too long to prepare anew, order a substitute entrée that can quickly be prepared.

TOASTS

Witty toasts at the beginning of the meal break the ice. Should you ever be at a loss for words, perhaps one of these classics will get your repast off to a congenial start:

I drink to your health when with you.
I drink to your health when alone.
I drink to your health so often
I now worry about my own.

May we be in heaven half an hour
Before the devil knows we're dead.
May we be out of this restaurant an hour
Before the waiter knows we've fled.

Here's to hell!
May our stay there
Be as much fun as the way there!

To our mothers' cooking:
May our wives never find out how bad it really was.

Here's to women—
once our superiors,
Now our equals.

I have known many,
    Liked few,
Loved one—
    Here's to you!

Let's drink to love,
Which is nothing—
Unless it's divided by two.

Here's to you, to me,
A consummate pair,
On this anniversary
Of our love affair.

6

Judging
the Food

Being critical does not mean disliking foods. The more you learn, the more shortcomings you will find, but—at the same time—the more pleasures you will discover in everyday fare.

Before you can competently assess food, you need to understand the roles played by your senses. You also need to know what you should be looking for when the waiter sets the food before you.

A SENSUAL PRIMER

You judge foods with five primary sensory mechanisms:

taste
smell
touch
sight
hearing

You also use these senses:

temperature
pain
kinesthetics
common chemical

Most people confuse *flavor* with *taste*. These two words are not synonymous. Flavor and taste are no more interchangeable than Pennsylvania and Philadelphia. The second word in each pair is a subunit of the first. Your sense of taste is limited in scope to what your taste buds can detect. Flavor is a composite term embracing taste, smell, and mouthfeel. (This last word describes the sensory responses other than gustation that take place on your lips and within your mouth. Touch, temperature, pain, kinesthetics, and the common chemical sense all help determine mouthfeel.)

French onion soup is my favorite vehicle for illustrating the multidimensional concept of flavor because that preparation can stimulate all nine types of receptors involved in flavor assessments. In a single spoonful you can experience the sweetness of onion (taste), the aroma of thyme (smell), the pungency of ground

99

peppercorns (pain), the warmth of the liquid (temperature), the sogginess of the floating toast (touch), and—as you slightly chew—the elasticity of the melted cheese (kinesthetics). If the soup was cooked in an old-fashioned cauldron, you can also detect iron through your common chemical sense.

You also use your sense of sight when you assess the visual appearance of the steaming soup in the bowl. Ears can come into play, too. In some cultures you are expected to make a slurping sound when consuming soup.

Your perception of the onion soup is the sum of the various impressions you receive simultaneously. Each sensory mechanism detects a different sensory property of the food and flashes its report to your brain.

Sweet, sour, salty, and bitter are your four basic types of taste buds. The sweet-responsive ones are concentrated on the tip, the sour and salty ones on the sides, and the bitter ones on the rear top of your tongue.

The sequence in which you taste the different foods can alter your sensory perceptions. If you take a bite of an apple before taking a sip of wine, the tartness of the wine will be magnified. Cheese, on the other hand, improves the wine's flavor. Hence this wine-merchant saying: "Buy on apples. Sell on cheese."

By closing your eyes, you can usually perceive more flavor and texture subtleties because visual distractions are eliminated. You can achieve nearly the same effect with your eyes open if you train yourself to give the food your full, undivided attention while eating.

To increase the perceived intensity of a food's scent without awkwardly leaning over the plate, directly face the dish with your head slightly tilted back. Then take a short series of quick sniffs.

Pay special attention to the first and last bite of a food. Generally, these two morsels give you the most enjoyment.

WHAT TO LOOK FOR

Discerning diners know how to spot culinary shortcomings. Here is a sampling of some of the indicators to look for when analyzing certain foods:

Baked Potatoes: These tubers should be fluffy and mealy, not mushy. This negative quality is the result of being baked in foil, cooked too long or too far in advance, not being pierced prior to baking, or using a boiling rather than a baking potato. Scorched or rotten spots are other common faults in a restaurant potato.

Barbecued Ribs: This popular finger food is often scorched, dry, stringy, and cloying—and excessively fatty.

Biscuits and Pancakes: A bitter taste suggests that the kitchen used too much baking powder to leaven the dough or batter. These foods should be light and airy, not leaden.

Cakes: Unsatisfactory cakes lack moisture and lightness, and are often too sweet.

Clams and Oysters on the Half Shell: The larger the bivalve for its species, the less sweet and tender it will be. The flesh should not be shriveled or discolored. The scent should remind you of a fresh sea breeze.

Cheese: Contrary to what some waiters would have you believe, the reek of ammonia is not a quality indicator. No cheese-loving Frenchman would touch such a specimen with a ten-foot baguette. He knows that the stench of ammonia is a sign of post-maturity rather than of maturity itself.

Chicken: If the meat is dry and stringy, the chicken was over-cooked. Redness around the bone does not necessarily signify an undercooked bird (the color comes from inside the bone, not the flesh).

Cooking Oil: Fried foods cooked in rancid oil will absorb its unmistakable rancid flavor (think of an old potato chip). An over-used oil can give off the odor of previously cooked foods. Unfortunately, cooking with off-flavored oil is the rule, not the exception, in restaurants.

Croissants: Reject one if it is greasy, soggy, crushed, or stale. The texture should be flaky and the flavor buttery (second-rate specimens are made with vegetable oil or margarine).

Crustaceans: Blandness, dryness, and excess water are never good signs for lobsters, crabs, and shrimp. The tail of a whole cooked lobster should be curled under its body (if it is not, it means the lobster was dead prior to cooking and therefore may be unhygienic). The claws of lobsters and crabs should be firmly attached when served. Shrimp with an iodine scent are suspect.

Curry: A curry blend should not be dominated by the biting, pungent flavor of the yellow rhizome called turmeric. The preferred primary coloring agent is the more expensive saffron.

Duck: A well-prepared roasted duck is not greasy. It is not bathed in a candy-sweet sauce.

Eggs: If you receive a rubbery fried egg, it was cooked at too high a temperature. If you see a green line between the yellow and white portions of a sliced hard-cooked egg, the egg was most likely boiled rather than simmered (as it should have been), or it was cooked too long. Such an egg will also emit a sulfuric scent. An omelette that is watery, flat, and dense is poorly made.

Fish: The flesh should not be mushy, watery, dried out, or scorched. It should be white (if applicable) and void of a fishy odor and petroleum taste. The latter attribute suggests that the fish was caught in a harbor teeming with motorboats. If filleted, the meat should not be shoddily boned. When ordering a whole fish, ask that the raw specimen be brought to the table for your scrutiny. Its eyes should be bright and clear, its body plump, its scent sea sweet, and its gills red.

French Bread: A good loaf has a chewy as opposed to cottony texture. Its internal air pockets are tiny. The bread has a thick crust.

French Fries: Poor ones are greasy, soggy, burnt, rancid, or oversalted. Some are made from rotten or sloppily peeled potatoes. French fries should be served hot and within ten minutes after they're made.

Frozen Entrées: If the interior of an entrée like a chicken breast has a cold spot, the food was probably frozen. The same is true if you see droplets of water (melted ice crystals) floating on top of the thawed sauce. An abnormally mushy texture is also a clue.

Garlic: A bitter flavor results when the garlic has been scorched. Garlic should never be sautéed for more than two or three minutes—and never at high heat.

Ham: The lower the grade, the more watery the texture and the more evident the chemical taste will be.

Hamburger: Deplorable burgers are compact, crumbly, and made with gristle-laden meat. A burger should be thick (for the sake of juiciness) and prepared from freshly ground beef.

Ice Cream: Quality ice cream melts slowly and has a creamy fullness. It should not have a chalky mouthfeel or chemical taste.

Lamb: For optimum tenderness and delicate flavor, lamb must not be cooked beyond the medium-rare state of doneness. A muttony aroma indicates that the meat is not from a young animal, which it should be.

Liver: If it is leathery, juiceless, and gray-hued, the liver is overcooked. Properly cooked liver has a rosy interior. Calf's liver is preferred to beef liver since it is more tender and subtly flavored.

Melons: If a melon lacks characteristic sweetness, the fruit is unripe and possible immature. Mushy flesh means the melon is past its prime.

Mussels: The mussels should be devoid of their beardlike growth. The flesh should be plump and sandless.

Onion Rings: If they lack texture, the onion rings are probably a factory product reconstituted from paste.

Pasta: If the pasta is pasty, it was very likely cooked too long, in too little water, or below boiling point. A low-grade brand is also a possible culprit. Pasta cooked *al dente* has a satisfying mouthfeel.

Pâté: You can distinguish a freshly made from a canned pâté because the latter will have a metallic note and be oversalted and laden with the type of chemicals associated with hot dogs and luncheon meats. A pâté is also substandard if it is grayish, dense, crumbly, greasy, bitter, or blandly or unevenly seasoned—or served refrigerator cold.

Pepper Mill: If the grinder is filled with low-grade peppercorns, the flavor will be harsh rather than relatively smooth and sweetly aromatic.

Pickles: A pickled cucumber should be vibrant green, not pallid or brownish. The texture should be firm and the taste not too biting, salty, or sugary.

Pies: The filling should not be runny (as are those made with commercially canned products). The crust should not be soggy, greasy, doughy, or scorched. With few exceptions, pies should not be served refrigerator cold.

Prime Rib: The largest and most tender prime rib is the one cut immediately next to the loin section of the steer (request that specific cut when you order). The least desirable prime rib is the steak cut nearest the chuck (shoulder) section.

Rice: The rice is overcooked if mushy, undercooked if the center of the grains are still hard. Rice should not be dried out (this indicates it has been cooked too far in advance). Neither should it have picked up a pot odor.

Salads, Iceberg Lettuce: The worst salad green is iceberg lettuce. Its surface is so impenetrable that all but the gooiest of dressings will easily slide off the leaves, collecting in a wasteful pool at the bottom of the bowl. Iceberg lettuce is also bland. Most chefs nevertheless use iceberg lettuce because it is less expensive and perishable than superior greens such as Bibb, Boston, and romaine. (Iceberg, however, does have a pronounced crispness which is desirable in sandwiches and tacos.)

Salads, Other: There are several causes for soggy salads: the washed leaves were not thoroughly dried prior to being tossed with the dressing; too much dressing was used; the salad was mixed too far in advance. For crisp leaves, the salad should be dressed no more than five minutes before it is served. A salad is inferior if it is gritty, too oily or vinegary, or made with poor-quality ingredients such as rancid or garlic-powdered croutons, greasy or artificially flavored bacon bits, and oxidized mushrooms.

Sauces: A taste of raw flour indicates an undercooked sauce. Those that are pasty, soupy, gummy, or too acidic, alcoholic, or sweet will never do justice to the entrée. Neither should the flavor of the sauce mask the food it is supposed to enhance (though some restaurants do it intentionally—for example, by camouflaging the unfresh flavor of shrimp, clams, or oysters with an overpowering horseradish-infused tomato sauce). A sauce from one preparation should not mingle with another food on the same plate.

Shish Kebab: These grilled specialties will be annoyingly chewy if made with gristly meat. Likewise if the meat comes from a less-than-tender cut of meat that was insufficiently marinated.

Smoked Salmon: Negative signs include paleness, mushiness, dryness, and excess saltiness. Meat from the belly is fattier, juicier, and more flavorful than that cut near the tail. However, you don't want the first few slices off the head end of the salmon. These pieces tend to be overly salty because as the salmon hangs by its tail during the curing process, the brine gravitates downward and concentrates.

Sole: All soles do not taste alike. A gray sole, for instance, is tastier than the less expensive lemon sole.

Soufflé: It should not be scorched or fallen or have an under-cooked interior. A soufflé is only as good as the quality of its filling or chief flavoring agent, be it cheese or chocolate.

Soups: Most of the soups I've encountered are bland (except for being oversalted), watery, and short of the featured ingredient. They are often made with chemically processed bouillon cubes or canned soup bases, served tepid, or taste like yesterday's dishwater. You can almost make an overall assessment of the quality of a restaurant by tasting this single dish because conscientious chefs take their soups seriously.

Squid and Octopus: A rubbery texture indicates it was over-cooked. The smaller the mollusk for its species, the sweeter and more delicate the flavor.

Steaks: Tenderness is only one of several qualities that a great steak should possess. Although a filet mignon may be fork tender, it may also be mushy and virtually flavorless because the restaurant or meat supplier used chemicals to tenderize the meat. If the steak was USDA Prime Grade, there would be no need to subject the meat to a dose of chemicals.

Stews: Substandard stews are floury or watery. The meat is often tough, stringy, and skimpy. Chefs usually overcook the vegetables and season the stew with a heavy hand.

Toasts: Burnt toast is not only distasteful and unappealing, it may be unhealthy. According to scientific studies, the carbon on burnt bread, muffins, bagels, or any type of food is carcinogenic.

Tuna Salad: A decent tuna salad should not be stretched with celery. Neither should it be made with an inexpensive canned tuna which is excessively oily and easily mashed.

Vegetables: Frozen vegetables tend to be mushy and faded (though frozen legumes like peas and green leafy vegetables like spinach suffer less damage). Canned vegetables are even worse and have a metallic taste. Fresh vegetables should be properly washed, trimmed, and cut. When cooked, they should not be soggy or wilted—or have lost their fresh farm flavor and vivid hue.

Whipped Cream: In many restaurants the "whipped cream" is neither whipped nor cream, and smacks of chemicals. Penny-pinching chefs use aerosol bombs with ingredients that read: water, partially hydrogenated vegetable oil, sugar, corn syrup, hydroxypropyl methylcellulose, artificial flavor, polysorbate 60, sodium stearoyl-2-lactylate, salt, mono- and diglycerides, artificial color. Nowhere in the above roll call is there any substance which came from a cow's udder.

OTHER POINTERS

The following tips and insights, which concern judging foods in general, should also prove helpful to you.

Herbs and Spices: Seasonings are designed to bring out and enhance the good natural flavors of the primary cooking ingredient. With a few exceptions, such as dill soup, a particular seasoning should not be too obvious. It should speak so unassumingly that you "hear" its individual flavor notes only when you make a conscientious effort to do so. Even in the case of blends like curry, no one aromatic spice—be it cumin, saffron, cardamom, or coriander seed—should overpower the other ingredients.

Whatever the combination of herbs and spices and other flavoring agents, it should not be used with a heavy hand, a transgression especially common among novice chefs. Neither should the chef be timid, as is the case in many restaurants which try to appeal to the broadest possible audience. In their attempt to please all, they excite few palates.

Variation is important, too. Rosemary is an excellent pan mate for lamb, but when any classic affinity becomes routine, the dish becomes routine as well.

Low-grade herbs have a grassy, haylike flavor. Their opposite numbers have a fresh, springlike quality.

Hot and Spicy Foods: I frequently hear diners say, "This is the best Sichuan food I've ever had—it's so hot." If quality is the equivalent of hotness, then a robot could be a gourmet Sichuan or Tex-Mex chef. It takes no particular talent to add more chilies to the pot.

Look for more than fire when you evaluate a dish. Each chili variety has its unique flavor, which should be apparent and fresh. Take into account the qualities of the other ingredients in the dish and their synergetic relationship.

There is an easy method, incidentally, to tell if a dish was served with chili peppers or peppercorns. The chili is significantly hotter and has a pronounced effect on the sensory receptors on the front of your tongue. A peppercorn's character is perceived mostly at the back of the tongue.

Detecting MSG: Regrettably, many chefs use MSG (monosodium glutamate). There is a way, however, to tell with just a single bite whether MSG has been used in a dish. All you need to do is to train your palate to recognize the distinct flavor that is produced when MSG chemically reacts with salt (most preparations contain salt). Conduct this experiment in your home: Half-fill three glasses with cold tap water. Stir ⅛ teaspoon of MSG into the first, ¼ teaspoon of salt into the second, and ⅛ teaspoon of

MSG plus ¼ teaspoon of salt into the third glass. Sample the first glass—note that unadulterated MSG is naturally tasteless. Take a sip from the second glass—note the natural salt flavor. Finally, sip the third glass of water. Not only will the chemical reaction between the salt and MSG amplify the salty flavor, it will also produce a metallic taste. This telltale note in a dish reveals the presence of MSG.

Cooled Foods: Restaurants that allow hot foods to cool to lukewarm temperatures are doing you a great disservice. The foods will be less flavorful and the sauces will prematurely congeal into unappetizing masses.

The causes of cooled foods are several. Perhaps the preparation was precooked and stored in a warming oven, over a water bath, or under a heat lamp that was insufficiently hot. (Even if the method used provided enough warmth, the food still suffers. Ultraviolet lamps, for instance, will quickly parch foods.)

Another possibility is that the food sat too long on the kitchen counter waiting for the waiter to fetch it. Or the food was served on an unwarmed plate (a cool platter rapidly absorbs heat from food).

Visual Appearance: The serving should be pleasing to the eye in terms of layout and color contrast. Foods on the plate should not overlap, as they usually do on a Tex-Mex combination platter.

Portions: Lilliputian servings are as despicable as Brobdingnagian ones. The first is tightfisted, the second gross.

The Pleasure Formula: I have noticed that the degree of dining pleasure often varies in direct proportion to a diner's expectations. The more you expect, the less likely you will be satisfied. This principle of human nature can be expressed in the following formula, where P stands for pleasure, Q for the quality of the dining experience, and E for the diner's expectations:

$$P = \frac{Q}{E}$$

For some other diners, pleasure is a self-fulfilling prophecy: the more money they spend, the better the food will seem.

Another pleasure variable is the people at your table. They can make a fine meal seem dreadful or a mediocre one divine. As I heard in Shanghai: "The devil gives us our relatives, but, thank the gods, we can at least choose our dining companions."

COUNTERFEIT ETHNIC FARE

Most ethnic eateries in America serve food that would be barely recognizable to the citizens of the native country. These establishments bastardize their culinary offerings in order to cater to the preconceptions, food biases, and bland palates of their typical American clientele. By appealing to the broadest common denominator, they let authenticity and flavor go out the window. Let us examine several of these malpractices.

You should be aware that some Chinese-American restaurants have two recipes for the same dish. If you are Chinese, the chef uses the authentic recipe. If you are non-Chinese and order sweet and sour pork, for instance, the sauce will probably contain extra cornstarch, which turns the coating liquid into the gummy mess that most Americans accept as standard.

It is difficult to find authentic Sichuan cooking in America. Most of the restaurants that call their cuisine Sichuan (or Szechuan) are merely Cantonese restaurants which have added some chili to their Cantonese-style dishes and then hung up a Sichuan Heaven shingle.

In the 1960s in Manhattan, a number of Asian-Indian restaurants opened, operated by Indians who knew little about cooking their native cuisine. One proprietor, for example, opened his establishment after he failed in his attempt to make a career in acting on Broadway. He had enough stage savvy to impress non-Indians, but seldom would you see even one Indian customer in his restaurant, because his food was monotonously curried and overcooked. The only thing *gas*tronomical I ever got in pseudo-Indian restaurants like his was the first three letters of that word. These unpalatable spots still proliferate in New York City, but I'm proud to report that today the Big Apple can boast several good Indian restaurants whose patrons include visiting Indian gastronomes.

Mexican-American restaurants, by and large, are deplorable. Their most popular specials are greasy combination plates on which the foods intermingle, giving you the flavor of everything and nothing simultaneously.

The restaurants which most Americans label authentic Italian are simply Neapolitan in scope—and poor examples of Neapolitan cooking at that. American diners by the drove swarm into their favorite Italian-American eateries and consume soapy-tasting spaghetti and meatballs, lasagna, ravioli, and veal parmigiana, washing it down with an inky bottle of third-rate Chianti that sits on a sauce-stained red-and-white-checked tablecloth. The culinary disasters can be seen only by the flickering light of a dripping candle stuck into a straw-covered wine bottle. On the wall is the mandatory painting of a Venetian gondola. Fortunately for the Italians who live in Naples, they don't have to eat in restaurants of this sort.

Most of the French bistros in America are one part Paris and two parts Hollywood. Their decor and menu are so alike that you can dine in several of them without having seemed to change restaurants. Before walking into one of these establishments, I can almost visualize its clichéd menu:

Coquille St. Jacques
Escargot de Bourgogne
Pâté Maison
Ratatouille
Quiche Lorraine
Soupe à l'Oignon
Vichyssoise [invented in America]
Sole Meunière
Grenouilles Provençale
Coq au Vin
Canard à l'Orange
Boeuf Bourguignonne
Steak Pommes Frites
Steak au Poivre
Mousse au Chocolat
Pêche Melba
Crêpes Suzette
Brie
Camembert

These specialties can be deserving *if well made,* but the French culinary culture has much more to offer the world than these stereotyped items.

7
Making
the Grand Exit

By knowing the ins and outs of departing a restaurant, you can eliminate unpleasant "with-
drawal symptoms." This chapter gives you
down-to-earth advice on topics such as tipping,
paying the check, asking for a doggy bag, and
getting reimbursed for your lost raccoon coat.

THE CHECK

Ask the waiter, never the busboy, for your check. Don't ask the captain unless this supervisor happens to be at your table.

To beckon a distant waiter with a snap of the fingers is always offensive. It is permissible, however, to signal your request by discreetly signing the air in front of you with an imaginary pen.

It's acceptable for a coffee-shop waiter to give you the bill along with the coffee. Not so in a restaurant—even on a bustling Saturday night. Should a restaurant waiter try to expedite your departure with the unsubtle technique of presenting you the check before you have any intention of leaving, politely say you are not finished and would prefer not to be rushed. Bright waiters will get your message.

Sometimes you have the opposite problem: you can't get your bill promptly. The cause is not always inadequate service. On one occasion, for example, my waiter purposely delayed giving me the bill until my dinner guest had returned from the rest room. He knew, I presume, she was my date. Had he seen a wedding ring on her finger, I suspect he would have presented the check to me in her absence. Seasoned waiters know a law of human nature: A man tends to be a bigger tipper when he is with a date or a mistress than when he is accompanied by a wife.

Waiters should make a little more effort to determine who's treating whom. Because I'm a man, I'm often presented the check when female executives take me out to lunch. This is sexist, and my hosts have a right to be indignant. When tablemates are of the same gender and the waiter is not sure who should get the check, it will often end up in front of the oldest, best-dressed, or most distinguished looking person. What the waiter should do is to be alert to who made the reservation or requested the check. When in doubt, the waiter should make a discreet query.

Check the check. Diners who don't like to scrutinize their bills for accuracy, because they don't like math, may end up disliking the aftermath. In my experience, roughly one out of twenty bar and restaurant bills is inaccurate; faulty itemizations or additions, bill padding, and inadvertent switches do occur.

Should you be charged for a food or beverage item you rejected? In most locales you are legally obligated to pay if the manager considers the food quality satisfactory. However, only a shortsighted restaurateur would force a disgruntled customer to fork over the money.

I've heard of a small restaurant in Sanger, Texas, where you don't get a check. The menu informs you: "When you have finished your meal, put whatever you desire in the jar on your table. And if you cannot pay, please take what you need." Nice. But it will never work in my neighborhood.

COMPETING FOR THE CHECK

"No, let me pay" is one of the most boorish games played at the dining table. It happens when the guest protests a host's right to be the gracious host. It also occurs in situations when no one is clearly the host. The tablemates argue relentlessly for the privilege of paying the check, while each secretly hopes that he or she won't be the last to say, "Aw, come on, this one's on me." Unless a diner is with a group of friends who have a tacit understanding that everyone takes turns paying the check, it usually makes sense for everyone to agree to split the tab equitably. Unfortunately, some people are too proud to do it.

TIPS ON TIPPING

Whether we like the multibillion-dollar institution of tipping or not, we must accept it. Gratuities constitute the predominant share of the wage structure of two million restaurant employees. On the average, tips account for two-thirds of a waiter's take-home pay.

Let me make one point clear: I don't feel obliged to tip for blatantly inferior service. Though, if the truth be told, it requires at least a modicum of courage on my part to withhold scratch. I just make certain that the waiter knows my motive lest he think I'm a miserly nontipper and thus the object lesson would be lost.

If the service is mediocre but not abominable, I reduce my tip to a suitable degree. On the other hand, if a waiter has performed beyond the call of duty (for example, by mopping up my spilled wine), I increase my gratuities fittingly. In the long run, my tips average out.

Never punish the waiter for the faults of the chef. When you get poor food but good service, tip for the good service. If dishes are slow in coming, try to ascertain whether the delay is being caused by the kitchen or the dining-room staff.

Extravagant tipping is just as inappropriate as stingy tipping. Though an excessive outlay gains the waiter's toothsome smile and makes the diner feel like a big shot, a "big spender from the East" loses the respect of the staff.

If you are a regular and spontaneously decide to leave a larger tip than usual because you are in high spirits, you run the risk of creating an ongoing problem. Your normal tip might not have the same impact as before.

A small but growing number of American restaurants are adopting the European custom of adding an automatic 15 percent or more service charge to the bill. If so, you needn't leave a tip on top of this surcharge—unless you receive an extra service that would justify your largess.

Another innocent but common form of overtipping is basing the gratuity on the after-tax total. Figure your tip on the pretax sum.

In modest eateries, you round off the tip to the nearest nickel in favor of the staff (eighty-one cents becomes eighty-five cents). In better establishments, the gratuity is rounded off to the nearest quarter, half dollar, or—in exclusive restaurants—dollar.

Sometimes diners give cash tips rather than post them to the credit-card slip because they believe the waiter will be more pleased. That is true. However, if the tips are pooled or shared with the busboys, this practice displeases other staff members. Costaffers feel assured of receiving their fair share when the tip becomes a matter of record on the credit card. From a diner's point of view, a noncash tip may be better for your financial records and your cash flow.

Beware of tip hustlers; their tricks of the trade are legion. For instance, they will try to spur you into leaving a liberal tip. Waiters will deliberately return your change in the largest possible denomination, giving you, say, a dollar bill and a dime in change for your five dollars. Don't be intimidated—coolly ask for smaller change. Another ploy is for waiters to glance down at your tip as if to say, "Is that all?" Ignore these finaglers.

Should the management give you a complimentary meal out of friendship or to curry your favor, you must still tip the staff. Base your gratuities on the estimated dollar value of the meal.

For many diners the most confusing aspect of the tipping protocol is trying to figure out how much to leave the maître 'd, captain, and waiter. Part of the problem stems from not being able to distinguish who's who. For a crash course, see the section "Identifying Who's Who in the Dining Room" on page 000 in Part Two, "Getting VIP Treatment."

Now for the specifics:

Proprietor: Traditionally, owners are never tipped, even if they are serving you in the role of maître d' or chief cook and bottle washer.

Maître d' (also known as the headwaiter): In a sophisticated restaurant, you do not tip this tuxedoed commandant. Exceptions to this rule are when you are trying to cultivate the restaurant, when you are a regular, or when you have asked the maître d' to arrange a special meal or banquet for you. Regulars should occasionally and discreetly give some green thank-yous to the amount of 2 to 3 percent of the pretax and -tip cost of their cumulative meals. Hosts of special dinners and banquets should use the same percentage to calculate the gratuity, usually bestowed on the maître d' just before or after the function.

What about maître d's working in nightclubs and pretentious restaurants? Unfortunately, they expect you to palm them two to ten dollars per chair for "selling" you a choice table or leapfrogging your name on the reservation list. Tipping in that genre of eating establishment sometimes, if you pardon the expression, gets out of hand.

Captain: Should a restaurant have a captain and should this employee assist you, tip 20 percent of the bill, but divide this percentage as follows: 5 percent for the captain and 15 percent for the waiter. Specify that the money is to be divided on a three-to-one basis. Otherwise, custom dictates that the whole tip goes to the waiter. When using a credit card, indicate the split on the slip.

Waiter: Tip the waiter 15 percent. If you are in a first-class restaurant and there is no captain, tip your waiter 20 percent.

Busboy: Leave nothing. Waiters traditionally turn over about 15 percent of their gratuities to the busboys.

Buffet Staff: When you serve yourself from a buffet, leave 5 to 10 percent of the tab on your table.

Coffee-Shop Personnel: Tip 15 percent at the table (minimum twenty-five to fifty cents) and 10 percent at the counter (minimum twenty-five cents). Delivery boys get about 10 percent (minimum twenty-five to fifty cents, depending mainly on the distance traveled). It's unnecessary to tip takeout waiters, but if you are a regular, an occasional dollar bill is appreciated.

Fast-Food and Cafeteria-line Employees: Don't tip. Frequent customers, however, should give these workers a cash gift at Christmas.

Wine Steward (Sommelier): Should there be a wine steward, tip this person one dollar per bottle or 10 percent of the bottle price, whichever is greater. Be sure to subtract the price of the wine from the bill when you are calculating the tip for the waiter and captain—otherwise, you'll be leaving a combined 30 percent tip for the wine.

Cocktail-Bar Attendant: Tip 15 percent (minimum twenty-five to fifty cents per person).

Musician: You need tip the piper (one dollar per request) only if you call the tune—or if you encourage with words or smiles a strolling musician to linger at your table.

Rest-Room Attendant: Tip twenty-five to fifty cents if you receive a towel or other service. Note: The attendant who keeps a conspicuously placed dish garnished exclusively with dollar bills would like you to believe that big tips are the norm.

Cloakroom Attendant: Give twenty-five to fifty cents per person, one dollar in an exclusive restaurant. The hatcheck personnel are often paid by the hour and the management winds up with the tip. Consequently, think twice about overtipping in response to a sexy wink. Don't tip if the restaurant charges a checking fee (unless you ask the attendant to keep a special eye on your property).

Doorman: A twenty-five-to-fifty-cent-tip is in order if the doorman performs a service such as hailing a cab. Opening the door to the restaurant does not count.

Valet Parking Attendant: Hand over two quarters to two dollars, depending on the class of the establishment and your car. You need not tip the attendant at a commercial parking lot or garage unless you are a frequent customer.

CREDIT CARDS

Did you know that credit-card frauds exceed one billion dollars a year? There are ways to keep yourself from becoming one of the victims. If the waiter says that an error was made and the cashier had to tear up your signed credit-card invoice, demand to see the mutilated evidence before you sign the new slip.

Keep your charge-slip copy to cross-check the figures when you receive your monthly bill. It's no secret that a few disreputable restaurant people alter the numbers—such as the amount of the tip. Other shysters make two impressions of your credit card and, a couple of months later, submit the second slip with a near-perfect forgery of your signature. They are hoping you will say to yourself, "I thought I paid that bill, but I guess I didn't."

PAYING WITH CASH

If you are paying with cash and want a receipt, ask for it when the waiter takes your money. This courtesy saves the waiter a trip.

PENNILESS

Sooner or later you will be presented the check only to discover that your wallet was lost, stolen, or left at home. Don't waste time by telling your sad story to the waiter. Ask to see the person in charge, the one with the authority to say, "Yes, you can pay me later." State your predicament in a confident tone. If the restaurateur won't take your word, offer to leave your hundred-dollar Stetson cowboy hat, Rolex watch, or gold earrings as collateral. Even if you have no valuables, you will not have to wash the proverbial dishes—unless you look like a derelict. Restaurateurs want your future business.

DOGGY BAGS

I'm in favor of doggy bags. It is wasteful to leave perfectly good food on your plate that will end up in a garbage can in an alley behind the restaurant. Yet some people are embarrassed to ask for one. When they do, they claim it's for a four-footed friend. You and I know that this pet seldom tastes filet mignon leftovers.

Most restaurateurs respect customers who request doggy bags. First, it's a compliment to their chef, and, secondly, a doggy bag is an opportunity for management to create goodwill. Some proprietors go as far as to emblazon their logos on the bag, presumably to impress Fido that its owner goes only to the swankiest restaurants.

Just about the only place it is improper to ask for a doggy bag is in a smorgasbord-type restaurant. Given human greed, doggy bags could bankrupt these establishments.

A RESTAURANT'S LIABILITY

Don't let a restaurant get off the hook too easily if it loses your coat even if the proprietor posts a Not Responsible sign. Check your local laws. In many municipalities, including New York City, the establishment is financially liable in whole or in part for your checked article.

Your case is strongest when the restaurant charges a checking fee. Some judges consider a displayed tip tray to be tantamount to a checking fee. Your case is practically nonexistent when you place your property on a self-service hook or rack.

Should a waiter spill catsup on your Dior gown (or caviar on your jeans), the restaurant should offer to pay the cleaning bill or compensate you for damages, whether or not the local statutes require this action. If the owner refuses to set matters right, tell your friends—and their friends. This hash house deserves all the bad word of mouth you can spread.

8

Coping with
Special Situations

*Special dining situations require special tips and
insights, whether you are entertaining business
clients, eating on the road, traveling abroad,
dining alone, dieting in a restaurant, feasting on
a shoestring, bringing the kids, amusing your
visiting Aunt Rhoda, hosting a foreign visitor,
romancing a lover, brunching in style, going to
the theater, being a dinner guest, attending formal banquets, enduring institutional food, dealing with MSG maniacs, or saving a choking victim.*

ENTERTAINING BUSINESS CLIENTS

Most of this book—and particularly Part Two, "Getting VIP Treatment"—is germane to entertaining business clients. This section passes along some additional tips and insights that specifically apply to business dining.

Let's examine tax deductions first. According to current IRS guidelines, you can write off your "three-martini" lunch if you meet these criteria:

1. The cost must be ordinary for your type of business.
2. The expenditure must be necessary for your particular business.
3. Some relevant aspect of business such as negotiations, selling, or gaining useful information must take place during (or just before or after) the meal. You do not necessarily have to make a sale, but you need a purpose stronger than merely building goodwill.
4. You must keep a diary or other written record specifying the place, time, and cost of the meal; the purpose of the meeting; the names and business relationships of those at the table (spouses of your guests are usually deductible.)
5. If the expense is twenty-five dollars or more, you must also have a receipt giving the date of the meal, the amount of the charges, and the name and address of the restaurant. This document can be the restaurant's receipt or the credit-card charge slip. The IRS does not always look upon a canceled check as an acceptable substitute for these receipts.

A Roman philosopher wryly observed, "Non exstat prandium gratuitum." This maxim, "There is no such thing as a free lunch," holds true today, especially for Uncle Sam, who gets stuck for half the ten-billion-dollar annual tab. You might say that expense-account dining is one of the government's biggest food programs, in the same league as school lunches and food stamps. Is this "subsidy" fitting and proper?

Most business lunches do conribute to the American economy. A meeting in a restaurant is better suited for some business encounters than an office meeting. It allows executives to meet on neutral turf, relax their guard, analyze each other's character at an unhurried pace, establish a common ground, brainstorm and explore ideas away from the pressures of the office, and gain a change of venue which helps freshen their outlook and nourish the psyche. The net result is better business decisions. And when the executives spend their lunch period conducting business, they are adding an extra hour or two to the workday.

The elimination of the tax deductions would have a direct and immediate impact on our economy. Thousands of restaurants would go broke and hundreds of thousands of restaurant employees would lose their jobs.

Perhaps the best argument for the continuance of the tax deductions is that cost-conscious corporations would be the first to pull the plug if it were not a legitimate business expense. After all, the second half of the tab is paid by these corporations out of their profits.

Choose the restaurant judiciously, because it reflects your taste—you are where you eat, particularly in the world of business. Your choice is also a measure of the esteem in which you hold your client or prospect—and you can be sure that most of your guests will draw silent conclusions.

Do not, however, take your guests where they might feel out of place or uncomfortable—that would be counterproductive. I know many business people who would rather eat ordinary fare in a nondescript eatery than dine in a posh French or Northern Italian restaurant.

Entertaining guests in a restaurant that demands sophistication beyond their level can backfire on you in yet another way. Your guests might ask the waiter in your favorite four-star French restaurant for a bottle of catsup.

The more important the guests are to you, the more you'll want the restaurant to be geographically convenient to them. But do not go overboard. If you can reduce your traveling time to a restaurant by ten minutes in each direction, you will gain, in the course of a year, the equivalent of approximately two weeks of extra work time in your office.

Select an establishment where you are known, even if it is not the best restaurant in town. Your guest will probably be more impressed with the deferential treatment you get from the waiter and chef at your humble haunt than the raised eyebrows you receive from the haughty maître d' at an unfamiliar restaurant.

Should your business tête-à-tête require confidentiality, select a restaurant where the tables are well spaced. The seating should not be so cramped that you feel you are an actor in an E. F. Hutton commercial, with nearby diners bending an ear to hear what you are about to say.

Private clubs and corporate dining rooms are very conducive to business discussions. Usually the waiters are less obtrusive, the decor is more subdued, the tables are more spacious, and the food plays a less starring role than in commercial establishments. A particular advantage of your company's having its own dining facilities is that your competition won't know whom you are hustling. On-premise dining rooms also give guests the cozy feeling that they are eating in someone's home.

The poor executive's private dining room is the office desk or, when it is available, the conference room down the hall. Though these work-in lunches save time and money, they are fraught with problems. Taking everyone's order can be tedious when you or your secretary has to jot the notes of a half-dozen versions of:

> I want roast beef on toasted rye—no, make that untoasted white bread—with Russian dressing on the side, but hold the butter and go easy on the tomato and lettuce. I'll also have tea with lemon on the side, but no sugar. Ask them if they have rice pudding. If not, get me a peach pie.

After foraging through brown paper bags for everyone's order, you probably won't be able to find Joe's ham and cheese sandwich. The coffee, naturally, will be bitter and served in those abhorrent Styrofoam cups. You'll be provided with undersized plastic spoons for your lukewarm soup. Naturally, there won't be enough napkins, so food and drinks will soil your clothes and business papers. And at the conclusion of the meeting, your desk will be an unsightly dump heap. Next time, dine out.

Breakfast meetings are gaining in popularity, especially in big cities like New York, Chicago, and Los Angeles. Generally, they take place in the dining rooms of luxury hotels or private clubs. Business breakfasts give busy executives an extra hour to transact business or swap inside information—and without telephone interruptions. These early-bird confabs tend to be more businesslike than lunch or dinner meetings—the attendees quickly get to the point. I know several power brokers who love business breakfasts so much that they schedule two on the same morning, one at 7:00 A.M. and one at 8:00 A.M.

There are some unwritten rules that every executive should know. If you are entertaining someone you are meeting for the first time, you normally do not get down to brass tacks until you are at least halfway through the meal. This waiting period extends over several meetings in the Japanese culture.

It is tacky to conspicuously display business papers at the table in a first-rate restaurant or club. Should the nature of your get-together necessitate showing documents, choose a more casual eatery where the perusal of business papers won't affront the sensibilities of nearby diners.

If you are meeting someone at a restaurant and you do not know what he or she looks like, give the appropriate details to the maître d' either orally or on the back of your business card, with instructions to show the other party to your table as soon as this person arrives. Otherwise, you run the risk of having the two of you dining alone at separate tables, impatiently waiting for each other to show up.

What to do if your dining partner is late? My rule of thumb is to wait until I have finished one leisurely drink. I then attempt to reach the person or my office by telephone to determine if there has been a mix-up or delay. Should my attempt fail, I usually go back to my table and start ordering my meal, one course at a time. If the person turns out to be a no-show, I have at least enjoyed the repast. If, on the other hand, I decide to forgo the meal and leave after a reasonable period, I write a suitable message for the absentee on the back of my business card and leave it with the maître d'.

When you are the guest, be wary of ploys pulled by unscrupulous seasoned diners. For instance, they will try to throw you off balance by asking you striking questions the moment you take a bite of food. Or conspiring executives will have a standing arrangement with the restaurant staff to make your drinks stronger than theirs. After a few drinks, you may find yourself revealing or agreeing to more than is prudent. Yet other schemers try to make themselves seem like big shots by having their secretaries call them at the restaurant with an "urgent message."

Expense-account abuses and falsifications are rampant. When a bill is too big to justify two diners to the boss, artful dodgers will list three people on their expense reports. Should they be dining with a friend for fun, they pull a fictitious name out of a hat or list the name of a cooperative business associate. Some executives patronize certain massage parlors over others because these establishments put the charges on credit-card slips bearing the name of real or imagined restaurants.

EATING ON THE ROAD

Dining on a trip can be an ulcerous nightmare. Or—if you know the secrets of veteran travelers—a pleasant adventure.

Airline Food: Tired of the same old bland airline fare? Have you had it with reheated and overcooked, mushy pot roasts and rubber chicken legs buried in gloppy sauces; wilted salads;plasticlike string beans; stale rolls; army-style scrambled eggs; cloying desserts? You have two alternatives: special-order your meal or bring your own.

Unbeknownst to most passengers, nearly all the major airlines will serve you a special meal for medical, dietetic, religious, philosophical, ethnic, or other personal reasons. These meals are, in most cases, more interesting than standard coach fare. In the course of my travels and for the sake of research, I have sampled these on various domestic and international airlines:

bland (for ulcers)	infant's meal
chef's salad	kosher
children's special	lacto-ovo vegetarian
deli sandwich	liquid
diabetic	low-calorie
fresh fruit	low-carbohydrate
gluten-free	low-cholesterol
high-protein	low-fat
Hindu	low-lactose

low-salt   salt-free
Mormon   seafood platter
Moslem   strict vegetarian
Oriental   sugar-free

Your travel agent or the airlines reservation operator can give you a rundown of the special meals available for your particular flight. Be sure to ask.

You have to order your special meal in advance—usually twenty-four hours before the pilot flashes on the Fasten Seat Belt sign. It's wiser, however, to make your request when you book your seat reservation. Computer foul-ups occur, so reconfirm your meal reservation with the ground personnel when you check in at the airport and with the cabin attendant when you step aboard the plane.

Quality standards vary from day to day, airline to airline. The broccoli on the vegetarian platter can be fresh and bright-hued or dull and soggy, depending on your luck.

Don't try to circumvent in-flight food by eating in airport restaurants. Since they cater to a captive audience on a monopolistic basis, these establishments can get away with serving lowly fare at sky-high prices. Your best bet is to bring your own food.

I frequently assemble a bring-along snack or meal to enjoy on long flights. In the past, I've packed foods like apples, caviar, cheese, cherries, cold lobster, empanadas, French bread, grapes, Greek olives, Nova Scotia salmon, pâté, peaches, pears, poached shrimp, Smithfield ham, and smoked turkey breast that I purchased at delicatessens and gourmet shops. A bottle of decent wine is also a worthy item for your gastronomic survival kit. An in-flight picnic beats typical airline food and helps alleviate the boredom of being confined for hours in a metal tube.

Cruise-Ship Food: The day of the glorious shipboard meals on the *France* and other grand ocean liners is sinking. Most of today's cruise ships design their culinary offerings to please the eye more than the palate because nearly all their passengers equate gaudy buffet displays with quality. These voyagers seem fixed on consuming a month's caloric intake in a week, and usually succeed.

Health standards are sickening on some ships. Passengers by the scores have been stricken with gastrointestinal illnesses because of shortcomings such as malfunctioning refrigeration and water chlorination systems. Several years ago the U.S. government made health inspections on seventy-three world-class liners. All but four were cited for violations. One ship failed twenty-one of twenty-two inspections.

The message is clear. Select the ships with the best reputations—and, even then, don't expect paradise.

Railroad Food: The greatest pleasure of dining on a train is the matchless, ever-changing view. Occasionally there will be a dedicated chef in the dining-car kitchen who somehow manages to cook tempting meals from scratch in the confines of a tiny, jolting, closet-sized chamber. Most of the modern trains, however, have button-pushing chefs who reheat frozen entrées. A sensible option is to bring your own food or buy a sandwich in the buffet car.

Highway Food: I have crossed this country a dozen times by car and learned there is an alternative to eating at the greasy-spoon and fast-food joints lining the highways. Carry in your trunk a cooler and a picnic basket complete with disposable plates, utensils, cups, glasses, and napkins; corkscrew and paring knife; salt, pepper, and condiments like mustard. I found that locally purchased bread, cheese, cold cuts, and sausages—such as Kielbasa made by local Polish butchers for their demanding Polish-American clientele—is perfect for an alfresco roadside picnic.

Should you be journeying by bus, you can still assemble a small cache of goodies to eat on the bus or on a grassy knoll while your fellow travelers jostle with each other for a seat in one of those bustling highway eateries that cater to the gobble-and-go set.

Forget the bromide "Truck stops are the best places to eat on the highway." All the truck drivers I have interviewed told me that quality in food is not their primary consideration for selecting an en route eatery. A higher priority is having adequate space to park their rigs. Moreover, after many long hours on the highway, the drivers are looking for a restaurant where they can share road talk with other truckers. At most of these pit stops, portion size is more carefully attended to than quality. And, as owners of these highway eateries know, a sexy waitress can be a bigger draw than Mom's perfectly cooked apple pie.

Finding the Best Restaurant in Town: Promotional signs can give you a clue to the quality of a restaurant. Establishments that boast "good food" or "home cooking" are usually disappointments. An ethnic name on a storefront augurs well—it's not a sure bet, but it's better than flipping a coin.

Though many travelers do, I never ask a cabdriver for a restaurant recommendation. Most hacks give honest but unqualified answers. Neither do I consult giveaway entertainment guides. They merely tout their advertisers.

What is a reliable source of information? Put your trust in an authoritative and impartial restaurant critic or in local acquaintances who know their onions. Concierges of leading hotels will not necessarily guide you to the finest restaurant, but their clout will help you get a reservation and a choice table.

Be prepared for regional differences. California wins the award for having the friendliest service and the freshest vegetables. Manhattan offers the greatest variety of ethnic fare but, regrettably, has the surliest waiters and the most expensive tabs. People eat relatively early in the Midwest. Order a "hero" in Boston, a "submarine" in Jersey City, and a "hoagy" in Philadelphia and you'll get the same type of sandwich. If you order "regular coffee," you will get it black in the South but laden with cream in New England.

TRAVELING ABROAD

One of the best ways to familiarize yourself with the people of a foreign land is to experience the local cuisine. Sometimes, however, you face more than the language barrier in pursuing this goal.

Turista, Montezuma's revenge, Delhi belly, Turkey trots, Inca two-step, or whatever you call traveler's diarrhea is a constant threat to any roaming gourmet. According to recent medical studies, more than one-third of the Americans who travel to Mexico fall victim to this malady. Many of the afflicted become bedridden or are forced to change their travel plans.

This peril, which is usually caused by the *Escherichia coli* or *E. shigella* bacterium, is greatest in poor cities, rural areas, and underdeveloped countries. The risk increases in direct proportion to the hotness of the climate and weather.

Despite the fact that my profession entails traveling to faraway lands to sample the native foods, I seldom get diarrhea. My secret, in part, is to heed these basic health precautions:

- Don't drink the local water unless it has been chlorinated or otherwise properly treated by the municipality or hotel. Be leery of hotels or restaurants that merely say that they boil the

water—to kill pathogenic microorganisms, water should be boiled for a full twenty minutes.
- Drink quality brands of bottled water that have been opened in front of you. Alternatives include beer, wine, and, if necessary, name-brand soft drinks (the latter can increase your thirst).
- Many travelers erroneously believe that hot coffee and tea are automatically safe. Germs can still thrive in water that was boiled for only a short time.
- Since a small quantity of imbibed contaminated water can cause diarrhea, don't brush your teeth with tap water in unhygienic areas. For the same reason, you shouldn't swim in unchlorinated pools.
- Order drinks without ice cubes and try to examine the glass beforehand—it should be thoroughly washed, rinsed, and dried.
- Forgo salads and undercooked vegetables and rare meats. Eat only fruits that you peel yourself, and wash your hands before eating finger foods (premoistened towel packets are handy).
- Avoid dairy products such as ice cream if made with unpasteurized milk, a potential carrier of tuberculosis.

Should you get traveler's diarrhea despite these precautions, most doctors recommend that you rest, eat sparingly, drink plenty of fluids, and—if the illness is severe or persists for more than a few days—consult a physician. Most of the popular drugs for treating dysentery are not nearly as effective as the old standby bismuth subsalicylate (the best-known brand is Pepto-Bismol). A new, promising pharmaceutical drug is trimethoprim, which can cure diarrhea in twenty-four hours.

Constipation, another traveler's affliction, is often the result of a change in diet. When people go on vacation, they tend to eat more meats, fats, and highly processed carbohydrates like white bread than they do at home. They should be eating ample amounts of fruits, vegetables, and whole grain foods for their roughage value.

Health is not the only problem for the peregrinating gourmet. It is difficult to find a restaurant in an underdeveloped country that serves foods that are both superbly prepared and authentically local. The reason is that there are rarely enough customers to support such establishments. The poor cannot afford them, and the rich eat excellent native food in their own homes (they have skilled peasant cooks who work for a song). When the well-to-do eat out, they want to sample something exotic—French or Chinese cuisine, for example. Most tourists seldom venture beyond the Continental-style dishes served in hotel dining rooms.

When hotels and tourist spots serve native dishes, the preparations are almost invariably redesigned to suit bland tastes. Moreover, these establishments love promoting ersatz local specialties. I've seen "Steak à la Caribbean" featured on a menu in Barbados even though the meat had to be imported to this tropical island in a frozen state. It would be better for you to sample dishes made with ingredients that are reared, harvested, or caught in Barbados—conch, for instance. You can always eat frozen steak at home, and for less money.

If you want to sample good authentic local fare, you may just have to visit someone's home. Besides, a country's cuisine is usually best judged in the house of a native, not in a restaurant.

One of the few countries that has an abundance of superb restaurants is France. However, some travelers are guilty of overkill. I know people who dined in all the three-star restaurants during their four-day stay in Paris. Their escapades were the wining and dining equivalent of a "nine European countries in eleven days" tour, and no doubt their recall of the culinary palaces was a cordon blur.

While you are dining in one of Europe's most illustrious restaurants, its famous chef may be several thousand miles away— perhaps in your hometown. Many French chefs like Paul Bocuse seem to spend almost as much time globetrotting on the PR circuit than in their kitchens. They are off plugging their latest books, opening spin-off restaurants, or signing deals to put their names on kitchen equipment, wine, and even frozen foods.

The costs of eating vary drastically around the world. You can enjoy a feast in Sri Lanka for $1.00 a head and a glass of beer in Norway for $6.00. On the edge of the Sahara in Timbuktu, I paid $10.00 for a liter of bottled drinking water (about $2.50 per glass). A quartet of visiting diplomats reputedly shelled out more than $1,000 for an ordinary meal in wartime Baghdad.

Food often tastes better in memory than in fact. This may help explain why that out-of-the-way trattoria in Florence that you dined in five years ago did not live up to your expectations when you recently revisited it.

Eating customs are different abroad. You are expected to sip soup directly from the bowl in Japan. In China, you raise the rice bowl to your lips and proceed to shovel the contents into your mouth with chopsticks. Burping at the end of a meal is considered a compliment to the host in some lands. Eating with your left hand is bad manners in India. How do you deal with these cultural idiosyncrasies? As the saying goes, "When in Rome, do as the Romans do."

Culinary names familiar to Americans can be confounding. Order a Spanish omelette in Spain and you will get a round egg pancake. Danish pastries are known as Wienerbrod (Viennese bread) in Denmark. Russian dressing is not Russian. Neither are chop suey and fortune cookies Chinese (they are American). Be ready for surprises.

DINING ALONE

Solitary dining is an occupational hazard of traveling executives and salespeople. Too often you are given a table behind the potted plant only to face a waiter who openly despises you for inhabiting a table that could produce two tips.

If your waiter wants you to leave quickly to make room for a couple, you will be served your soup, entrée, dessert, coffee, and check in rapid succession. Otherwise, you might be ignored—the interlude between courses will be as long as waiting for a bus on a street corner at 3:00 A.M.

Women face added problems. Often they are either patronized or treated as unwelcome patrons by maître d's and waiters. They are harassed by boorish men who make suggestive remarks and think that they can buy them with a drink.

The much-abused single diner should follow these tactics:

• Seek interesting diversions—for example, by eating in an outdoor café that has tables well situated for people watching. Some diners find discreet eavesdropping equally exciting.
• Avoid restaurants with a romantic or intimate ambiance. They tend to make solo diners feel lonely.
• If you are in a garrulous mood, visit a restaurant where you can sit elbow to elbow with other diners. Sushi bars, community or "captain's" tables, and long banquettes are ideal.
• If you are going to be isolated by choice or circumstance, select a restaurant with interesting food. Many ethnic restaurants fit the bill.
• Make reservations. Self-confidently say, "a table for one," instead of the apologetic-sounding "only for one."

- If an acquaintance knows the maître d', ask this person to make the reservation for you.
- Dress well—this will help assure you an accommodating reception.
- Should you be treated as a second-class customer—for instance, by being assigned an undesirable table—politely but firmly demand your due.
- Don't accept the restaurant's profit-oriented suggestion that you share a table with a stranger unless the idea appeals to you. A sure way to lose your appetite is to sit facing a dullard or a chatterbox.
- A woman's best defense against macho staffers and obtrusive male diners is to deal with them in a self-assured and assertive manner. Sadly, some women sidestep the sexist problem by eating in crowded coffee shops or in their lonely hotel cell where room service typically arrives late, lackluster, and lukewarm.
- Be your own guest—indulge yourself as much as your diet and pocketbook allow.

Some restaurants have an unwritten policy that they turn down reservations for singles on busy nights. I know of some solo diners who beat the system by booking a reservation for two, then—when seated—moan to the waiter, "Oh, it looks like my date stood me up."

DIETING IN RESTAURANTS

Weight-watching myths are as numerous as dumplings in a Czech restaurant. Some of the most prevalent fallacies are:

"Gourmet food is fattening." People are always asking me, "If your profession is eating food, why aren't you fat?" I discovered long ago that it is mediocre, not gourmet, foods that put on weight. Ever notice how quickly and inattentively people eat a high-calorie junk food like a bag of potato chips? Put a culinary masterpiece in front of them, however, and they eat more slowly and thoughtfully. Equally important, they usually will consume far fewer calories because quality dishes are more satiating. Also, the memory of a fine repast easily tides you over until the next meal.

"All diet specials are low in calories." Some diet claims are

fraudulent. I recall one New York fast-food restaurant that advertised "Diet Freeze—only 60 calories." An independent laboratory test proved that the concoction actually contained 126 calories.

"Cottage cheese and frozen yogurt are diet foods." These items are two of the most overrated diet foods. Cottage cheese has 260 calories per cup, nearly twice that of whole milk. Many frozen yogurt products contain almost as many calories as an ice cream—and if you add those sugary granola and coconut toppings, the calorie count zooms.

"Nouvelle cuisine *is significantly less fattening than traditional* haute cuisines." Not so. By eliminating the roux (a blend of butter and flour) to thicken sauces, *nouvelle cuisine* chefs save only 20 calories per serving. Moreover, because the *nouvelle cuisine* chefs thicken their sauce by reducing the liquid, the resulting product often has more calories per ounce than a traditional roux-thickened sauce. Most people don't realize that *nouvelle cuisine* chefs use a lot of high-calorie ingredients like heavy cream in their dishes.

"Grilled meats are okay if the chef withholds the sauce." Even sans sauce, you may still end up eating a slew of extra calories because most chefs liberally baste grilling meats with an oil or fat such as butter.

"The calorie count is equally low for all fishes." Oily fishes such as eel, mackerel, salmon, and rainbow trout have approximately twice the calories of lean species like cod, sole, sea bass, and red snapper.

"Bread, pasta, potatoes, and rice are fattening." What makes these welcome belly fillers a dieter's nightmare are the butter and rich sauces people customarily put on them.

"Dieters should order hamburgers without the buns." The calorie count of the average burger is 500 for the meat and 125 for the bun. Without adding a single calorie to their meals, dieters could have more interesting and filling lunches by simply leaving one-quarter of the burger (125 calories) and eating the remaining meat inside the whole bun.

"Dieters should drink white, not red, wines." The difference in calories between dry white and red wines is about 4 calories per ounce—that's only 16 calories per serving, the equivalent of just one-third pat of butter. Moreover, the typical white wine is sweeter than its red counterpart.

"Light wines are great for dieters." I do not think much of light wines. The mere 25 calories per glass they save you hardly com-

pensates for the bland, uninspiring flavor of these watered-down products. If you want to cut calories, do it in other areas where the savings are more substantial and the gustatory sacrifice less severe.

People on strict weight-reduction diets needn't forfeit the pleasures of dining out. They just have to select foods more judiciously than do more fortunate diners. First, they must get into the habit of asking the waiter questions such as "Are the vegetables buttered?" and "Can the chef serve the hollandaise sauce for the fish on the side?"

The best exercise for dieters is the pushaway: nudge your chair slightly away from the table before you feel sated. Though you may think you are still hungry, you have to give nature time. The message that your stomach is full takes twenty minutes to reach your brain.

Other tried and true techniques include forgoing fatty appetizers, ordering consommé instead of cream soups, pushing the butter plate beyond arm's reach, learning to appreciate tea and coffee without cream or sugar, and skipping dessert unless it's fresh fruit.

Don't despair. If you manage to lose an average of one-half pound per week, you will shed twenty-six pounds in a year.

FEASTING ON A SHOESTRING

Is there a pricey restaurant that you have always wanted to visit but have not because you think you cannot afford it? Take heart. Chances are you can if you employ these money-saving tips:

- Visit the restaurant for lunch because the cost of that meal in most establishments is approximately two-thirds that of the dinner price.
- Take advantage of early-bird specials.
- Have your cocktails and postprandial drinks at home because alcohol can increase the cost of a meal by 50 percent. (Also review the money-saving tips discussed in the "Wine" section on pp. 55–57 in Part Four, "Choosing the Beverage.")
- Remember this German proverb: "He who keeps his eyes shut must open his purse." Before sitting down, scrutinize the menu and query the maître d'. You may discover, for example, that

the cut-rate fixed-cost meal limits you to a hackneyed table d'hôte dinner such as cream pea soup, roast chicken, and vanilla ice cream. Dishes of more than routine interest in this type of restaurant usually require surcharges.

- Unless you want a full meal, you are better off ordering à la carte than table d'hôte. The latter is no bargain when, for instance, you would normally have skipped the soup or dessert. Besides, the difference in price between ordering the table d'hôte special and the identical items on the à la carte list is sometimes so negligible that the saving does not justify your sacrificing freedom of choice. Occasionally the saving is nonexistent. I've seen menus where the tally of the à la carte items is less than the ballyhooed table d'hôte price.
- If the restaurant has a hefty bread-and-butter charge, ask if this supplemental cost would be waived if the waiter removed the bread and butter from the table. Many restaurants acquiesce—though, admittedly, some do it more gracefully than others.
- If you are willing to forfeit gastronomic variety, it is possible to eat in most luxury restaurants for a relative pittance. I've seen corporate presidents spend only ten dollars ordering a hamburger and a cup of coffee in the exclusive 21 Club, where dinners average about fifty dollars per person. Luncheon salads and omelettes are among the other comparatively low-priced items that are frequently available in deluxe restaurants. A more creative alternative is to order something kooky, such as a plain baked potato accompanied by a glass of dry Madeira garnished with a carrot stick. The waiter, thinking you are on a trendy new diet, will probably not even bat an eyelash.
- If you can't afford the food but want to experience the ambiance of a famous restaurant, drop by for a cocktail.
- Should you be hosting someone in a high-price restaurant and your guest is eyeing the exorbitant filet mignon, casually steer him or her in the right direction by casually remarking, "I understand the sole is great here."

When comparing prices of restaurants of equal quality, take into consideration portion size. One trick of the trade is to serve abnormally small amounts. By slicing the apple pie into seven rather than the traditional six slices, restaurateurs increase their revenue on that item by 17 percent. By cutting the pie into eight parts, they augment their apple-pie sales income by 33 percent without spending an extra penny.

Ethnic restaurants, for the most part, are well suited for dollar-watching diners. While establishments featuring classic Japanese, French, or Northern Italian cuisines can be prohibitively costly, those serving cuisines such as Chinese, Indian, Mexican, and Southern Italian should not scuttle too many budgets.

Fast-food outlets have low prices and generally do not require that you leave a tip. Quality is another matter (see the "Fast Foods" section on pp. 187–89 in Part Ten, "Potpourri").

Street vendors—a special type of fast-food operation—offer low prices, but buyer beware. The orange juice they sell in the heat of the day is often diluted with melting ice. Most of the foods are laden with chemicals. Food poisoning is a concern, too. Many mobile carts are ill equipped for keeping perishable foods like hot dogs and taco fillings sufficiently hot or cold to thwart bacterial contamination.

One of the best values is the ad hoc restaurant that you can easily set up in your local public park. It doesn't cost much money to pack a picnic basket full of homemade treats.

Some people practice an even less expensive way of eating out. They graze the mobbed bars that offer free hors d'oeuvres (not exactly a dietitian's dream) without buying a drink. Then there is the professional dining companion who is always quick to accept an invitation but slow to reciprocate.

I've seen pikers dining out free in my local supermarket. As they push their cart down the aisles, they open and eat packages of potato chips, cold cuts, and other comestibles. When glutted, they abandon the cart and carry their food home in their stomachs instead of in a grocery bag.

Of course, the ultimate freeloader is the restaurant critic. He or she eats and gets paid for it.

BRINGING THE KIDS

These pointers are for parents new to the dining *en famille* experience:

• Do not take children to a formal restaurant until they have learned how to cope with more casual eateries. Otherwise, they will not feel comfortable and relaxed.

- Be prepared for a cool reception from some of the maître d's of luxury restaurants when you arrive with youngsters in tow. Experience has made these black-tied staffers a bit paranoid.
- Dining out should be fun for the child. However, it's a two-way street. Some parents seem to be oblivious to the effect that crying or troublesome children have on other diners. Though no one could reasonably expect that parents could make their child behave like a perfect angel, there is little question that in a first-class restaurant parents would be inconsiderate of other diners if they did not take their bawling baby out of the dining area or try to restrain their rambunctious moppet.
- Avoid those spots with long, drawn-out service. The interim between courses in those restaurants can seem like an eternity to a youngster.
- Recognize that children will probably eat less in an unfamiliar environment than they will at home. Your argument that you spent twenty-five dollars on their Dindonneau Montmorency will not convince them that they should finish their dish. (A promise of a dish of ice cream might, however.)
- To save money, ask if the restaurant has special plates or a menu for children. If not, ask if the children can split an adult-sized portion or share your entrée (if so, instruct the waiter to bring an empty plate).
- If possible, do not dine later than the children's accustomed eating hour. Should it be necessary, give the child a snack beforehand. Dining before a restaurant's peak hours has a special advantage: you get a broader choice of tables (perhaps one with an adjacent parking space for the stroller).
- Your children will not stagger out of the restaurant from eating wine-flavored foods. Cooking evaporates the alcoholic content of spiked dishes.
- Encourage your children to experience new foods. Unless you expose them to culinary variety and excellence early in life, they may reach adulthood as fast-food graduates (the child's taste is the father of man's). However, do not force them. You seldom can win a convert to a new food in a single meal. Suggest that your child take a single bite of your dish; then let it be. Sooner or later, your children will acquire a taste for the finer foods in life.
- Set a good example by showing a genuine appreciation for the food you are eating.

- Be an educator. Explain the various dishes and their significance.
- Never tell your child, "You won't like it" (as many parents do). This attitude becomes a self-fulfilling prophecy and creates unadventuresome palates that eventually atrophy beyond redemption.
- On special occasions such as a child's birthday, select the restaurant to please his or her and not your taste. No two kids have exactly the same gustatory cravings, but most have a predilection for these entrées: spaghetti, spare ribs, shish kebabs, crêpes, veal parmigiana, batter-dipped fish or chicken, pizza, hamburgers, and finger foods in general. Favorite categories of restaurants include ethnic-style operations such as Chinese, Polynesian, Tex-Mex, smorgasbord, Neapolitan, and Japanese-style steakhouses. Wild West decors, puppet shows, musicians, and magicians are popular, as are clowns or costumed waiters who give away free balloons, hats, lollipops, and other paraphernalia. Finally, remember that kids prefer restaurants that are teeming with other kids.

AMUSING YOUR VISITING AUNT RHODA

You may dislike touristy restaurants, but they could be the perfect cup of tea for your visiting Aunt Rhoda from Backwater, U.S.A. It is a well-established fact that the Aunt Rhodas of this world prefer famous names, kitschy decors, and cornball menus over epicurean fare, so why not let them have their fun? Suggest they eat in those restaurants on the days when you cannot accompany them.

HOSTING A FOREIGN VISITOR

We Americans have such an inferiority complex about our native cuisine that we are more apt to take those foreign visitors who have sophisticated palates to a French restaurant than to an eatery that features American cooking. Why not ask your foreign guests whether they would like to experience American food? They probably will give you an emphatic yes; they eat in enough French restaurants when they are at home or traveling through France.

Whenever you have the opportunity to entertain foreigners, take them to a restaurant that features and prepares good (but not necessarily fancy) regional American food. Alternatively, take them to a first-rate steakhouse, an American institution, and order these three culinary specialties that are without peer anywhere else in the world: charcoal-grilled USDA Prime Grade steak, baked Idaho potato, and corn on the cob. Eat on the side a farm-fresh salad, and don't forget to order a quality California Cabernet Sauvignon wine. If you follow my recommendations, your visitors will return home proclaiming: "America has good food!"

ROMANCING A LOVER

Through trial and error the great lovers of the world have discovered the ideal restaurant ambiance for romancing a lover. Look for a spot that corresponds with the scenario outlined below. Though this setting will not guarantee you a passionate denouement, it will increase the odds for success.

- Lighting is muted and indirect. The color of the gently flickering candles—which are everywhere—is pastel amber rather than bleached white or blatant red.
- Your table is covered with virgin-white linen which sets off the polished silverware, glistening bone china, and oversized crystal goblets. Fresh flowers, generous in perfume, harmonize with the colors in the spotlighted oil paintings gracing the walls.
- Carpets and drapes have a rich yet subdued hue. Red, which is fine in rooms with wood-paneled walls, should not be overused, as is the case in many cliché romantic hideaways.
- Your table is a corner booth for two, private yet well situated so your eyes can absorb the dining-room ambiance. The seats or chairs are soft and cozy, just the right size and height to make you feel relaxed and comfortable.
- When you are not talking, you hear the dulcet hum of tranquil conversation and the refined tinkling of quality tableware. Should there be music, it is a love song professionally performed by a low-keyed pianist, string instrumentalist, or crooner.
- Your clothes are stylish and as sexy as the occasion and restaurant allow. You are not wearing green, loud hues or busy pat-

terns (they can create anxiety) or a watch (timepieces evoke the pressing problems of life).
- You feel secure in this restaurant, partly because the staff treats you with respect. Service is efficient but not intrusive. Waiters are tactful (more than one couple has broken up because an indiscreet waiter asked, "Will your wife be having the same drink she had last Friday night?").

The Foxy Seducer: A decade ago a Midwest restaurant offered what was called a Snow Job Special for sexist male customers who wanted to impress their dates. The patron paid in advance a $60 fee which included all costs: food, drink, tax, and tip. When he arrived at the restaurant with his date, who was unaware of the conspiracy, he received a royal welcome and the best table in the house. He and his date were handed menus; clipped to each was a sheet listing $25 soups, $100 entrées, and $50 desserts. He ordered them along with a "$300" bottle of ordinary red wine suggested by the wine steward. During the meal, the maître d' came over to the table, complimented him on his urbane tastes, and asked him for advice on how to run the restaurant. At the conclusion of the meal, he magnaminously scribbled "$150 tip" and his signature on the phony check and was kowtowed out of the restaurant by the maître d'.

There are other ploys available to sly seducers. I know several schemers who analyze the menu, searching for dishes concocted with ingredients possessing reputed aphrodisiac properties. These edibles, which the seducer believes will increase his or her dining companion's sexual hunger and performance, include:

allspice	chili pepper
apricots	cinnamon
artichokes	dates
asparagus	eels
avocados	egg yolks
bananas	frog's legs
basil	ginger
caraway seeds	ginseng
caviar	honey
cherries	leeks
cheese fondue	lobsters
chocolate	mace

mangoes	saffron
mushrooms	sage
oysters	scallops
papayas	sesame seeds
passion fruit	sheep's testicles
peaches	shrimps
quails	truffles
rosemary	vanilla

Some foods—such as the phallic banana and carrot—are supposed to arouse the female but stifle the male's sexual urge. The cherry tomato and the suggestively shaped fig do just the opposite, some believe.

In the beverage department, the cordial—whose name derives from the latin word for *heart*—has long been considered a sexual stimulant. Cognac, champagne, and elegant red wines also have centuries-old reputations as aphrodisiacs.

One of the wiliest seducers I know told me that she could predict the outcome of the evening by observing how her dining partner ate. "Great lovers," she tattled, "eat their food sensuously. Pickers tend to be stingy in bed. Fast eaters are in and out of the sack like a rabbit."

BRUNCHING IN STYLE

Brunch derives its name from a combination of breakfast and lunch because it is, in its authentic form, exactly that. It was originated in New York City about half a century ago by late-Saturday-night revelers who didn't roll out of the sack until midday Sunday. Apparently they couldn't decide whether they were in the mood for breakfast or lunch, so they created a happy compromise. The now-traditional alcoholic drink accompaniment gave them the excuse to "bite the hair of the dog that bit them."

The original 11:00 A.M. to 2:00 P.M. Sunday time bracket has been stretched. Some establishments serve brunch from as early as 10:00 A.M. to as late as nightfall, on both Saturdays and Sundays. Generally, the most fashionable time to arrive on the scene in sophisticated cities like San Francisco is about 1:00 P.M. on Sundays.

Be adventurous by going beyond the cliché brunch dishes (eggs Benedict and cheeseburgers with french fries are the most trite of all). Hackneyed brunch drinks include watered-down Bloody Marys and screwdrivers. Lively ambiances are better than sedate ones, but avoid settings with last night's stale smoke and blaring TV sets (unless your favorite team is on the tube). Select a place that accepts reservations—it's no fun standing in a line squandering precious sunny weekend hours looking at the back of someone's head, especially if you drank like a drowning brontosaurus the night before.

GOING TO THE THEATER

I have never enjoyed eating a full dinner in a restaurant before attending the theater. It's not easy to relish food or your companion when you are keeping an eye on your watch, counting the minutes to curtain time. Furthermore, your hurried or anxious mood may cause you to develop a slight case of indigestion which hampers your concentration on the performance. Result: you end up not fully enjoying the meal or the play, or both.

When I go to the theater, I prefer to either limit myself to a light, casual, and unrushed meal like a sandwich beforehand, or wait to have a grander repast after the final curtain.

On the rare occasion when I do dine before the theater, I follow certain rules for my stomach's as well as the waiter's sake. I arrive at least two hours before curtain time, order only those dishes which don't demand lengthy preparation, and tell the waiter up front that I must leave at a certain time to catch the opening curtain.

BEING A DINNER GUEST

Technically, when you are eating in someone else's home you are dining out, so I've included this section. It's been my experience that the most inconsiderate deeds guests commit concern punctuality, gifts, volunteering, and table etiquette.

Being tardy to a sit-down dinner is particularly rude because it throws the host's culinary timetable out of kilter. Even those people who enjoy being fashionably late should arrive no later than fifteen minutes after the designated time.

If you want to bring the host a bouquet of flowers or a bottle of wine, be sure it will be a welcome gift. Flowers, which usually necessitate the host's rummaging through the cupboards for a suitable vase and arranging the blossoms, can be a burden if the host happens to be putting the finishing touches on the meal. If you are uncertain of the host's last-minute workload, arrange to have the flowers delivered in advance.

Presenting a bottle of wine on the threshold might be insulting because it can imply that you are more capable than the host in selecting the best wine for the meal. On those occasions when you feel it is correct to bring wine, ask the host beforehand what he or she will be serving. (Should one of your guests arrive with an unexpected bottle of wine, you are under no social obligation to serve it that evening. If it doesn't dovetail into your meal plan, simply thank the donor and say you look forward to enjoying the wine at another meal.)

Before going into someone's kitchen, you should ascertain whether the host wants your help or presence. Some do, many don't.

At a small dinner party, do not start eating until the host or hostess takes the first bite. If there are more than four (some say six or eight) people at the table, it is usually permissible for you to start eating before everyone else is served. Otherwise, the food would get cold.

You don't have to try everything. If you don't like something that is offered to you, politely refuse it.

One formal dinner party rule which has largely gone by the boards but which is still retained in some circles is "turning the table." When guests enter the dining room, the males help seat the females to their right and the couples chat until the middle of the dinner. At this point the hostess signals that "the table must turn" by beginning a conversation with the male on her right. After the hostess changes conversation partners, everyone else follows suit and the table is effectively "turned."

You'll find other pointers on manners in the "Table Etiquette" section on pp. 83–89 in Part Five, "Eating the Meal."

ATTENDING FORMAL BANQUETS

About the only type of formal banquet I thoroughly enjoy is that held for ten diners around a large circular table in a Chinese

restaurant. Keys to success include a gifted chef and knowledgeable tablemates who can appreciate his or her culinary
genius. Punctuality is also critical because dishes or the chef's
enthusiasm should not be allowed to cool or wither. I heartily
subscribe to this Chinese saying: "People wait for food; food
should never wait for people."

Most of the offerings served at gourmet functions held in ball-
rooms are glorified hotel banquet items. Were it not for the fact
that the meat in your Suprême de Poulet aux Concombres was
delivered today rather than yesterday, it might have ended up as
the proverbial rubber chicken at the sports awards dinner that
was held in the building on the previous evening.

Victuals served at functions conducted in large restaurants generally share the same destiny. The demands of serving so many
guests the same food at the same time force the kitchen staff to
use volume recipes and to prepare most of the food ahead of time.
You end up with reheated mass-produced provender.

Even at the ceremonious dinner of the Confrérie des Chevaliers
du Tastevins that is held annually at the Clos de Vougeot castle in
Burgundy, the fare is gastronomically disappointing. When I
noticed that the kitchen on the premises was too ill-equipped to
feed the multitude who attended this function, I asked one of the
organization's officials how on earth the mission was accom-
plished. He confessed to me that some of the food was cooked in
kitchens distant from the walls of this famous vineyard and was
simply trucked in.

A friend of mine hauled me off one night to attend the annual
gourmet game dinner of the Yale Club of New York (yes, even
Harvard men are on occasion allowed to tread on that hallowed
ground). I had rosy expectations because the offerings were to
include elephant, bear, kangaroo, lion, hippopotamus, elk, and
gazelle meats; all came from sources that did not violate then-
existing endangered species regulations. The chef delivered the
goods, but unfortunately the meats had obviously arrived in his
kitchen in a canned or frozen state. What he had to cook he
overcooked.

Buffets at formal events such as at weddings and state recep-
tions are usually gastronomic disasters. There is, however, one
type of buffet which sometimes produces exceptionally delicious
treats: the potluck dinner at a church social. Despite the
preacher's Sunday-morning exhortations on behalf of Christian

behavior, the contributing cooks to the potluck dinner compete viciously with each other to produce the most sinfully good dishes.

ENDURING INSTITUTIONAL FOOD

When forced to eat in army mess halls, college cafeterias, hospitals, or prisons, your chances of improving your gastronomic lot are virtually nil unless you go AWOL, drop out of school, or make the great escape. I'm afraid captive audiences will always be at the mercy of bureaucratic kitchen administrators.

DEALING WITH MSG MANIACS

Whenever you suspect that a restaurant uses monosodium glutamate (MSG), tell the waiter, "Absolutely no MSG." The flavor created by the chemical reaction between salt and MSG gives foods an unnatural taste.

Should the waiter forget to tell the chef, and the dish arrives smacking of the substance, send it back. (To learn how to detect the presence of even a small dose of MSG, see "Detecting MSG" on pp. 106–07 in Part Six, "Judging the Food").

Some diners meticulously shun Chinese eateries because they believe they would otherwise get an MSG-induced headache (this affliction is known as the Chinese Restaurant Syndrome). Granted, a megadose of MSG will make anyone's head painfully throb. Yet the amount of this flavor enhancer used by even the most inept of Chinese chefs is usually too small to cause a headache in anyone except the small percentage of the population that is genuinely hypersensitive to MSG. For the rest of the people who get headaches whenever they eat in a Chinese restaurant, the symptoms are largely psychosomatic: these individuals think they're supposed to get a headache, and they do.

Individuals who are hypersensitive to MSG suffer from what is called a vascular headache. The MSG compound dilates the blood vessels, which then exert pressure against the pain receptors in the head. Swelling vessels also cause the facial skin to blush.

If you are hypersensitive to MSG and love eating Chinese food, be sure you visit only the quality restaurants—and by quality I do not necessarily mean expensive. The chefs in these establishments use little or no MSG.

Unless you are positive that the dish you order will not contain MSG, I suggest you avoid those containing mushrooms. Some scientific studies indicate that a compound in mushrooms can magnify the potency of MSG.

An MSG-sensitive diner should also avoid most coffee shops and second-rate restaurants in general. The cooks in these spots often add MSG to their dishes as indiscriminately as the worst chefs in Chinatown. (Incidentally, the major carrier of MSG is the processed food sold in supermarkets.)

SAVING A CHOKING VICTIM

This book would be incomplete if it did not have a section on saving the life of a choking victim. Each year hundreds of diners needlessly die in restaurants because no one present knew how to handle the emergency. By learning how to perform the relatively simple Heimlich Maneuver for adults and large children as outlined below, you may someday save a life, perhaps your own.

Café coronary, as this accident is sometimes called, occurs when a piece of meat or other object becomes lodged in the throat. Unless the victim is aided, he or she will likely die in about four minutes. You must act promptly.

It is critical that you do not misdiagnose the emergency. The symptoms of a choking victim are clear. The sufferer desperately clutches his or her throat, is unable to breathe or speak, and will start turning blue and eventually lose consciousness. If the victim can talk or breathe, he or she is probably experiencing a different type of crisis such as a heart attack.

The Standing Position: If the victim is conscious or can be lifted, use this (or the sitting position) technique:

- Stand behind the standing victim.
- Wrap your arms around the victim's waist.
- Make a fist with one hand. Position it so that your thumb is against the victim's abdomen between the navel and the rib cage.
- Grasp your fist with your free hand.
- Using a quick backward-upward thrust, pull your covered fist into the victim's abdomen (your goal is to dislodge the obstruction in the throat by forcing air out of the lungs into the windpipe).
- Repeat this maneuver as often as necessary. Use increased force on each attempt.

The Sitting Position: Basically, this maneuver is identical to the standing one except that the victim is in a chair while you stand or kneel behind it.

The Supine Position: Should the victim be unconscious and cannot be lifted, use this technique:

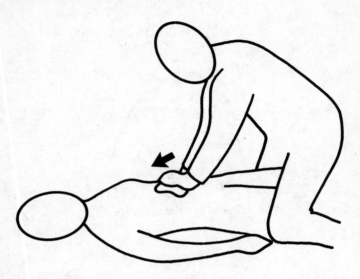

- Roll the victim on his or her back.
- Kneel over the victim by straddling his or her thighs.
- Place the heel of one of your hands on the victim's abdomen between the navel and the rib cage.
- Cover that hand with your free hand.
- Using a quick downward-forward thrust, press your covered hand into the victim's abdomen.
- Repeat this maneuver as often as is necessary. Use increased force on each attempt.

The Self-Help Technique: Perform the standing maneuver on yourself by pulling your covered fist into your abdomen with a quick backward-upward thrust. Repeat if necessary.

Once the obstacle is cleared, a set of car keys is usually the best first-aid item. Rush the victim to a doctor for examination for possible internal injuries.

9
Translating French and Italian Menus

This section of the book will help you cope with the next French or Italian menu that's thrust into your hands.

I've gathered the terms from menus I have perused throughout France and Italy. These languages were chosen because you are more likely to encounter French and Italian menu terms in America—even in nonethnic restaurants.

You will find both lists reasonably comprehensive: abricot *to* zingara *in French and* abbacchio *to* zuppa inglese *in Italian. Nevertheless, they are by no means all-encompassing. For either cuisine, it would take an entire volume to present a complete menu dictionary.*

Because space is at a premium, I have concentrated on several hundred single-word food names and descriptions as opposed to several thousand appellations of basic dishes. With this system, it is easy to decipher most multiword entrées simply by translating each word. Tête de veau *on a French menu, for example, is "head of veal" (calf's head).*

For your convenience, I also give phonetic pronunciations. The translations of a few items, such as the French noun for melon, *are obvious. I've included them for no other reason than to furnish you with their proper pronunciations.*

FRENCH MENU TRANSLATOR

abricot (ah-bree-koh′): apricot.
agneau (ahn-yoh′): lamb.
aigre (eyg'ruh): sour.
aigre-doux (eyg'ruh-doo′): sweet and sour.
ail (eye): garlic.
aile / aileron (ehl / ehl-rahn′): wing.
aïoli (eye-oh′-lee): garlic-infused mayonnaise.
à la / à l' / au / aux (ah lah / ahl / oh / oh): in the style or manner of;
   with.
alcool (ahl-kahl′): spirits.
Allemande, à l' (ahl-eh-mahnd′) German style.
alose (ah-lohz′): shad.
Alsacienne, à l' (ahl-zah-s'yehn′): in the style of Alsace.
amande (ah-mahnd′): almond.
ananas (ah-nah-nah′): pineapple.
anchois (ahn-shwah′): anchovy.
ancienne, à l' (ahn-s'yehn′): in the old style.
andouille (ahn-doo'ee′): tripe sausage.
anguille (ahn-ghee′): eel.
arachide (ah-rah-sheed′): peanut.
Argenteuil (ahr-zhahn-toy′): implies the presence of asparagus.
aromates (ah-rohm-maht′): seasoned with flavorful ingredients
   such as herbs.
artichaut (ahr-tee-shoh′): artichoke.
asperges (ahs-pehrz′): asparagus.
assiette de (ahs-see'eht′): plate of.
assorti (ah-sohr-tee′): assorted.

aubergine (oh-behr-zheen'): eggplant.
avec (ah-vehk'): with.
avocat (ah-voh-kah'): avocado.
ballottine (bahl-loh-teen'): a boned, stuffed, and rolled meat.
banane (bah-nahn'): banana.
bar (bahr): sea bass.
barquette (bahr-kett'): a small, filled, boat-shaped pastry.
bavaroise (bah-vah-rwahz'): Bavarian cream.
béarnaise (bay-ahr-nehz'): a hollandaiselike sauce flavored with shallots, tarragon, and vinegar.
béchamel (bay-shahm-ehl'): a standard white sauce.
beignet (beh-n'yay'): a deep-fried fritter.
Bercy (behr-see'): a sauce made with shallots, butter, white wine, and broth.
beurre (buhr): butter.
bière (byehr): beer.
bifteck (beehf-tehk'): steak.
bigarade (bee-gah-rahd'): an orange-flavored sauce for duck.
bisque (beesk): a thick, creamy, puréed soup.
blanc (blahn): white.
blanquette (blahn-kett'): meat stewed and served in a creamy white sauce.
boeuf (boof): beef.
boisson (bwah-sohn'): drink.
bombe (bawmb): molded ice cream.
bonne femme, à la (bohn fahm): prepared in a simple country style (literally, "good woman").
bordelaisse, à la (bohr-dah-lehz'): Bordeaux style.
bouchée (boo-shay'): small, filled puff pastry shell.
boudin (boo-dehn'): a blood sausage.
bouillabaisse (boo-yah-behz'): Marseilles-style fish stew.
bouilli (boo-yee'): boiled.
bouillon (boo-yohn'): clear meat soup.
bouquetière (boo-keh-t'yair'): garnished with vegetables.
bourguignonne, à la (boor-geen-yahn'): Burgundy style.
bourride (boo-reed'): fish casserole.
braiser (bray-zay'): braised.
brioche (bree-ohsh'): a small yeast roll made with butter and eggs.
brochet (broh-shay'): pike.
brochette, à la (broh-shett'): on a skewer. Also: *en brochette.*
brouillé (brou-yay'): scrambled.
cabillaud (kah-bee-yoh'): codfish.

cacao (kah-cow'): cocoa.
café (kah-fay'): coffee.
café filtre (kah-fay' feel'truh): coffee brewed in a tabletop drip pot.
caille (kye): quail.
calmar (kahl-mahr'): squid.
canard (kuh-nahr'): duck.
caneton (kahn-tohn'): duckling.
cannelle (kah-nell'): cinnamon.
capres (kahp'ruh): capers.
carotte (kah-roht'): carrot.
carpe (kahrp): carp.
carré (kah-ray'): a rack of, for example, lamb.
carte, à la (kahrt): priced on a dish-by-dish basis.
cassoulet (kah-soo-lay'): a bean and smoked meat casserole.
caviare (kahv-yahr'): caviar.
céleri (say'l-ree'): celery.
cerise (suh-reez'): cherry.
cervelle (sehr-vell'): brains.
champignon (shahm-pee-n'yohn'): mushroom.
chapelure (shahp-lehr'): bread crumbs.
charcuterie assortie (shahr-koo-tree' ahs-sohr-tee'): assorted cold
    cuts.
charlotte (shahr-lott'): a filled molded dessert.
chasseur, à la (shah-suhr'): usually prepared with sautéed mush-
    rooms (literally, "hunter's style").
chaud (shoh): hot.
chaud-froid (shoh-frwah'): a dish which is cooked, then chilled for
    serving (literally, "hot-cold").
cheval (shuh-vahl'): horse.
chevreau (shuh-vroh'): kid (a young goat).
chevreuil (shuh-vroy'): venison.
chocolat (shoh-koh-lah'): chocolate.
chou (shoo): cabbage.
choucroute (shoo-kroot'): sauerkraut.
choufleur (shoo-fluhr'): cauliflower.
choux de Bruxelles (shoo duh broo-sell'): brussels sprouts.
cidre (seed'ruh): cider.
citron (see-trohn'): lemon.
civet (see-vay'): a game stew, often hare or rabbit.
cochon de lait (koh-shawn' duh lay'): suckling pig.
coeur (kuhr): heart.
compote (kohm-poht'): stewed fruit.

compris (kohm-pree'): included.

concombre (kohn-kohm'bruh): cucumber.

confit (kohn-fee'): meat (usually pork or goose) preserved in its own fat.

confiture (kohn-fee-teur'): fruit preserve; jam.

conserve (kohn-sehrv'): a food preserved in a jar or can.

consommé (kohn-soh-may'): a clear soup.

contrefilet (kohn'truh-fee-lay'): loin steak.

coq (kohk): roaster, or chicken in general.

coquille (koh-kee'): shell.

cornichon (kohr-nee-shohn'): small pickle.

côte (koht): rib chop.

cotelette (koht-lett'): small rib chop.

cotriade (koh-tree-ahd'): fish stew.

coulibiac (koo-lee-b'yahk'): flaky-crusted pie filled with, for example, salmon.

coupe (koop): cup.

courgette (khoor-zhet'): small green squash.

couvert (koo-vehr'): cover charge.

crabe (krahb): crab.

crécy (kray-see'): implies the presence of carrots.

crème (krehm): cream.

crème Chantilly (krehm shahn-tee-yee'): whipped cream.

crème fraîche (krehm frehsh): slightly soured, thickened cream.

crêpes (krehp): thin pancakes.

cresson (kreh-sohn'): watercress.

crevette (kreh-vett'): shrimp.

croissant (krwah-sahn'): crescent-shaped flaky pastry.

croque-monsieur (krohk-muh-s'yuh'): ham and cheese sandwich dipped in egg batter, then fried.

croquette (kroh-kett'): fried patty or ball of chopped food.

croustade (kroos-tahd'): a filled, deep-fried bread case.

croûte, en (kroot): baked in a crust.

crudités (krew-dee-tay'): raw vegetables served as appetizers.

crustacés (krew-stah-say'): shellfish.

cuisse (kwees): leg.

cuit (kwee): cooked.

darne (dahrn): thick fish steak.

datte (daht): date.

daube (dohb): braised or stewed meat.

daurade (doh-rahd'): flounder.

de / des (duh / day): of.

dégustation (day-gew-stah-s'yong'): a tasting of various dishes or wines.

déjeuner (day-zhuh-nay'): lunch.

demi (duh-mee'): half.

dessert (duh-sehr'): dessert.

diable (dee'ah'-bluh): deviled; highly seasoned.

dinde (dand): hen turkey.

dindon (dan-dohn'): tom turkey.

dindonneau (dan-dohn-noh'): young turkey.

dîner (dee-neh'): dinner.

divers (dee-vehr'): sundries.

double (doo'bleh): double strength.

doux (doo): sweet.

du Barry (doo bah-ree'): implies the presence of cauliflower.

duchesse (doo-shess'): garnished with creamy mashed potatoes.

duxelles (dewk-sehl'): a chopped mushroom mixture.

échalote (ay-shah-loht'): shallots.

écrevisse (ay-kruh-vees'): freshwater crayfish.

émincé (ay-mahn-say'): sauced, thinly sliced meat.

en (ahn): in; into.

entrecôte (ahn-truh-koht'): rib steak.

épaule (ay-pohl'): shoulder.

épices (ay-pees'): spices.

épinard (ay-pee-nahr'): spinach.

escalope (ehs-kah-lohp'): boneless thin slice of meat.

escargot (ehs-kahr-goh'): snail.

estouffade (ehs-too-fahd'): stewed meat.

estragon (ehs-trah-gahn'): tarragon.

esturgeon (ehs-tuhr-zhan'): sturgeon.

et (ay): and.

faisan (fuh-zahn'): pheasant.

farci (fahr-see'): stuffed.

faux-filet (foh-fee-lay'): tenderloin.

fermière (fehr-m'yair'): farm style.

feuilleté (fuhy-tay'): flaky "leaf" pastry.

fèves (fehv): large broad beans.

figue (feeg): fig.

fines herbes (feen zairb): a mixture of finely chopped herbs.

flageolet (flah-zhoh-lay'): small legumes resembling lima beans.

flambé (flahm-bay'); flamed with spirits.

flan (flahn): custard.

foie (fwah): liver.

foie gras (fwah grah): the liver of force-fed poultry (usually goose).

fond (fahn): the center or heart of a food.

forestière (foh-rehs-t'yair'): implies the presence of mushrooms, bacon, and potatoes (literally, "forest-ranger style").

four, au (fohr): oven-baked.

fraise (frehz): strawberry.

framboise (frahm-bwahz'): raspberry.

frappé (frah-pay'): iced.

fricassée (free-kah-say'): a stew of browned meat.

frit (free): fried.

froid (frawh): cold.

fromage (froh-mahz'): cheese.

fruits de mer (frwee duh mehr): seafood mélange.

fumé (few-may'): smoked.

galantine (gah-lahn-teen'): boned and stuffed meat (usually poultry).

garni (gahr-nee'): garnished.

gâteau (gah-toh'): cake.

gaufre (gohf'ruh): waffle.

gelée (zhuh-lay'): jelly.

gibier (zhee-b'yeh'): game.

gigot (zhee-goh'): leg (of lamb, for instance).

glace (glahs): ice; ice cream.

glacé (glah-say'): iced or glazed.

gras (grah): fat; fatty.

gratin / gratinée (grah-tahn' / grah-tee-nay'): a dish with a crust of grated cheese or bread crumbs.

grenade (gruh-nahd'): pomegranate.

grenouille (gruh-n'wee'): frog.

grillade (gree-yahd'): grilled.

groseille (groh-say'): currant.

haché (ah-shay'): chopped.

hareng (ah-rahn'): herring.

haricots vert (ah-ree-koh' vehr): string beans.

homard (oh-mahr'): lobster.

huile (weel): oil.

huîtres (wee'truh): oysters.

jambon (zhahn-bohn'): ham.

jardinière (zhar-dee-n'yair'): garnished with diced vegetables.

julienne (zhew-l'yehn'): with shredded vegetables.

jus (zhew): juice.

lait (lay): milk.
laitue (lay-tew'): lettuce.
lamproie (lahm-prwah'): lamprey eel.
langouste (lahn-goost'): large saltwater crayfish.
langoustine (lahn-goos-steen'): small saltwater crayfish.
langue (lahng): tongue.
lapin (lah-pan'): rabbit.
légumes (lay-goohm'): vegetables.
lentilles (lahn-tee'): lentils.
lièvre (l'yehvr): hare.
limande (lee-mahnd'): lemon sole.
limon (lee-mohn'): lime.
loup de mer (loo duh mehr): sea bass.
lyonnaise (l'yohn-nehz'): usually implies the presence of onions.
macédoine (mah-say-dwahn'): mixture of diced fruit or vegetables.
maïs (mah-ees'): corn.
maison, à la (meh-zohn'): in the style of the house.
maquereau (mahk-roh'): mackerel.
mariné (mah-ree-nay'): pickled; marinated.
marron (mah-rohn'): chestnut.
médaillon (may-dah-yohn'): small round slice of meat.
melon (muh-lohn'): melon.
meunière, à la (muhn-n'yair'): floured fish fried in butter.
miel (m'yehl): honey.
mijoté (mee-zhoh-tay'): simmered.
mille feuille (meel fuhy): flaky pastry (literally, "thousand leaves").
mimosa (mee-moh'-sah): garnished with chopped egg yolk.
mollet (moh-lay'): soft-boiled, as with eggs.
Montmorency (mohn-moh-rahn-see'): sour cherries.
morille (moh-ree'): a spongy, cone-shaped mushroom.
Mornay (mohr-nay'): white sauce with cheese.
morue (moh-rew'): codfish.
moules (mool): mussels.
mousse (moos): any of several light, frothy mixtures, as chocolate or fish mousse.
moutarde (moo-tahrd'): mustard.
mouton (moo-tohn'): mutton.
mulet (mew-lay'): mullet.
mûr (mehr): ripe.
naturel, au (nah-tehr-ehl'): cooked plain (literally, "natural").

navarin (nah-vah-rahn'): mutton or lamb stew.

navet (nah-vay'): turnip.

noir (nwahr): black.

noisette (nwah-zeht'): hazelnut; small round piece of meat.

noix (nwah): nut, particularly the walnut.

nouilles (noo'ee'): noodles.

oeuf (euhf): egg.

oie (wah): goose.

oignon (oh-n'yohn'): onion.

oiseau (wah-zoh'): bird.

olive (oh-leeve'): olive.

orange (ah-rahnz'): orange.

oseille (oh-zay'): sorrel.

ou (oo): or.

oursin (ohr-sahn'): sea urchin.

pain (pahn): bread.

palourdes (pah-loord'): clams.

pamplemousse (pahm'pleh-moos'): grapefruit.

pané (pah-nay'): breaded.

papillote, en (pah-pee-yoht'): enclosed and cooked in paper.

parmentier (pahr-mahn-tee'ay'): usually implies the presence of
    potatoes.

patate (pah-taht'): sweet potato.

pâté (pah-tay'): cooled and sliced loaf of seasoned ground meat.

pâtisserie (pah-tees'ree'): pastry.

paysanne, à la (pay-zahn'): in the peasant style.

pêche (pehsh): peach.

Périgourdine, à la (pay-ree-goor-deen'): in the style of Perigord;
    usually implies the presence of truffles.

persillad (pehr-see-yahd'): contains parsley.

petit (puh-tee'): small.

pétoncles (payt-onc'luh'): scallops.

pied (pee'ay'): foot or trotter.

pigeon (pee-zhohn'): pigeon.

pigeonneau (pee-zhohn-noh'): squab.

pignon (pee-n'yohn'): pine nut.

piment (pee-mahn'): pimento.

pintade (pahn-tahd'): guinea hen.

pistache (pees-tahsh'): pistachio.

plat du jour (plaht dew zhoor'): daily special.

poché (poh-shay'): poached.

point, à (pwahn): cooked to a medium stage.

poire (pwahr): pear.
poireau (pwah-roh′): leek.
pois (pwah): peas.
pois chiches (pwah sheesh′): chickpeas.
poisson (pwah-sohn′): fish.
poitrine (pwah-treen′): breast.
poivre (pwahv′ruh): black pepper.
pomme (pohm): apple.
pomme de terre (pohm duh tehr′): potato.
porc (pohr′): pork.
potage (poh-tahzh′): soup.
poularde (poo-lahrd′): roasting chicken.
poulet (poo-lay′): young chicken.
poulpe (pool′p): octopus.
primeurs (pree-muhr′): young; early (such as vegetables).
printanière (prahn-tah-n′yair′): served with young spring vegetables.
prix fixe (pree feeks): fixed price.
profiteroles (proh-feet′uh-rohl′): cream puffs.
Provençale, à la (proh-vahn-sahl′): in the style of Provence—
  usually with tomatoes, garlic, olive oil, and herbs.
prune (prewn): plum.
quart (kahr): quarter.
quenelles (kuh-nehl′): delicate dumplings of minced fish or meat
  bound with eggs and cream.
queue (kuh): tail.
quiche (keesh): pie shell filled with a savory custard.
radis (rah-dee′): radish.
ragoût (rah-goo′): stew.
raie (ray): ray; skate.
raifort (ray-fohr′): horseradish.
raisins (ray-zahn′): grapes.
raisins sec (rah-zahn′ sehk): raisins.
ratatouille (rah-tah-too′ee′): a stewed medly of garlic-seasoned
  garden vegetables with eggplant, tomatoes, etc.
rillettes (ree-yet′): a seasoned spread made with pork or goose
  plus fat.
ris de veau (ree duh voh): sweetbreads.
rissole (ree-sohl′): a tiny meat-filled pastry turnover.
riz (ree): rice.
rognons (roh-n′yohn′): kidneys.
romarin (roh-mahr-ahn′): rosemary.

rosbif (rohs-beef'): roast beef.

rosé (roh-say'): pink.

rôti (roh-tee'): roast meat; roasted.

rouge (roozh): red.

rouget (roo-zheh'): red mullet.

roulade (roo-lahd'): a slice of rolled, stuffed meat.

russe (roos): Russian style.

saignant (sah-n'yahn'): rare.

St. Germain (sahn zher-mahn'): implies the presence of green peas.

saison, de (say-zahn'): in season.

salade (sah-lahd'): salad.

salé (sah-lay'): salted.

salpicon (sal-pee-kohn'): cubed or diced and served in a sauce.

sandwich (sahnd-veesh'): sandwich.

sauce (sohs): sauce.

saucisson (soh-see-sohn'): sausage.

sauge (sohzh): sage.

saumon (soh-mohn'): salmon.

sec (sehk): dry.

selle (sehl): saddle (of lamb, for instance).

seltz (selts): soda.

service (sehr-vees'): service.

sirop, en (see-roh'): in syrup.

sole (sohl): sole.

sorbet (sohr-bay'): sherbet.

soupe (soop): soup.

specialité (speh-s'yahl-ee-tay'): speciality.

steack/ steak(stehk): steak.

sucre (soo'kruh): sugar.

supplément (soo-play-mahn'): surcharge.

sus, en (suhs): extra; additional.

tarte (tahrt): round, sweet-filled pie.

tasse (tahss): cup.

terrine (teh-reen'): baking container, often made of earthenware.

tête (teht): head.

thé (tay): tea.

thon (tohn): tuna fish.

thym (teem): thyme.

timbale (tahm-bahl'): drum-shaped, filled pastry shell.

tisane (tih-zahn'): herb tea.

tomate (toh-maht'): tomato.

tortue (tohr-too'): turtle.

tournbroche (turn-brohsh'): roasting spit.

tournedos (toorn-nuh-doh'): small slice of tenderloin.

tourte (toort): round meat-filled pie.

tout compris (too kohm-pree'): all surcharges included.

tranche (trahnsh): slice.

tripe (treep): tripe.

tronçon (trohn-sohn'): a piece, chunk, or slice of fish.

truffes (trewf): truffles.

truite (trweet): trout.

turbot (toor-boh'): large flat European fish, similar to halibut.

vanille (vah-nee'): vanilla.

vapeur, à la (vah-puhr'): steamed.

varié (vah-ree'ay'): varied; assorted.

veau (voh): veal.

venaison (vuh-nay-zohn'): venison.

véronique (vay-roh-neek'): garnished with grapes (literally, "Verona style").

vert-pré (vehr-pray'): implies a garnish of watercress (literally, "green-meadow style").

viande (vee'yahnd'): meat.

vichyssoise (vee-shee-swahz'): cold, creamy potato soup (invented in America!).

villeroy (veel-rwah'): food dipped in sauce and crumbs, then deep-fried.

vin (van): wine.

vinaigre (vee-nay'gruh): vinegar.

vinaigrette (vee-nay-greht'): oil and vinegar dressing.

volaille (voh-lye'): fowl; poultry.

vol-au-vent (vohl-oh-vahn'): pastry shell with a creamed savory filling.

xérès (zheh-rehss'): sherry.

yaourt (yah-oort'): yoghurt.

zingara, à la (zahn-gah-rah'): usually implies the presence of chopped ham and mushrooms, (literally, "gypsy style").

ITALIAN MENU TRANSLATOR

a (ah): at; in; to.

abbacchio (ahb-bahk'-kee'oh): baby or young lamb.

acciuga (ah-choo'-gah): anchovy (northern dialect).

acceto (ah-cheh'-toh): vinegar.

acqua (ahk'-kwah): water.

acqua minerale (ahk'-kwah mee-neh-rah'-leh): mineral water.

affogato (ahf-foh-gah'-toh): poached or steamed.

affumicato (ahf-foo-mee-kah'-toh): smoked.

aglio (ah'-l'yoh): garlic.

agnello (ah-n'yehl'-loh): lamb.

agro (ah'-groh): sweet.

agrodolce (ah-groh-dohl'-cheh): sweet-sour.

ai (ah-ee): at the; to the

al/alle/allo(ahl/ahl'-leh/ahl'-loh): to the; at the.

alice (ah-lee'-cheh): anchovy (southern dialect).

albicocca (ahl-bee-kohk'-kah): apricot.

all' / alla (ahl / ahl'-lah): in the manner or style of; to the; at the.

amatriciana, all' (ah-mah-tree-chee'ah'-nah): rich tomato sauce for pasta originating in the town of Amatrice.

ananas (ah'-nah-nahs): pineapple.

anguilla (ahn-gweel'-lah): eel.

animelle (ah-nee-mehl'-leh): sweetbreads.

anitra (ah'-nee-trah): duck.

antipasto (ahn-tee-pah'-stoh): hors d'oeuvre; appetizer.

aragosta (ah-rah-goh'-stah): spiny lobster (large saltwater crayfish).

arancia (ah-rahn'-chee'ah): orange.

arrosto / arrostito (ah-roh'-stoh / ahr-roh-stee'-toh): roast; roasted.

asciutto (ahs-chee-oot'-toh): dry.

asparago (ah-spah'-rah-goh): asparagus.

assortito (ahs-sohr-tee'-toh): assorted.

banana (bah-nah'-nah): banana.

basilico (bah-zee'-lee-koh): basil.

bevanda (beh-vahn'-dah): drink.

bianco (bee-ahn'-koh): white.

bistecca (bee-stehk'-kah): steak.

boccone/bocconcino (bohk-koh'-neh/bohk-kohn-chee'-noh): mouthful; small mouthful or tidbit.

bollito (bohl-lee'-toh): boiled.

bolognese, alla (boh-loh-n'yeh'-zeh): in the style of Bologna.

bottiglia (boht-tee'-l'yah): bottle.

braciola (brah-chee'oh'-lah): chop; rolled cutlet.

brasato (brah-sah'-toh): braised.

broccoletti di Brusselle (brohk-koh-leht'-tee dee brooz-zehl'-leh): brussels sprouts.

broccoli (brohk'-koh-lee): broccoli.

brodo/brodetto (broh'-doh/broh-deht'-toh): broth.

budino (boo-dee'-noh): pudding.

bue (boo'-eh): ox.

burrida (boor-ree'-dah): garlicky seafood soup Genovese style.

burro (boor'-roh): butter.

cacio (kah'-chee'oh): cheese.

cacciatore, alla (kah-chee'ah-toh'-reh): hunter style—with mushrooms, shallots, wild herbs, wine, and possibly tomatoes.

cacciagione (kah-chee'ah-jee'oh'-neh): game.

caffé (kah-feh'): coffee.

caldo / calde (kahl'-doh / kahl'-deh): hot; warm.

calamari (kahl-mahr'-ee): squid or cuttlefish.

calzone (kahl-zoh'-neh): pizza dough turnover stuffed with ham and cheese.

cannella (kahn-nehl'-lah): cinnamon.

cannelloni (kahn-nehl-loh'-nee): large pasta squares rolled around stuffing, topped with a sauce, then baked (literally, "large reeds").

cappelletti (kahp-pehl-leht'-tee): small stuffed pasta (literally, "little hats").

capelli d'Angelo (kah-pehl'-lee dahn'-jeh-loh): the thinnest of spaghetti (literally, "angel's hair").

capellini (kah-pehl-lee'-nee): extremely thin spaghetti (literally, "fine hairs").

capperi (kahp-peh'-ree): capers.

cappuccino (kahp-pooch-chee'-noh): hot coffee blended with milk.

capra (kah'-prah): goat.

caraffa (kah-rahf'-fah): decanter.

carbonara, alla (kahr-boh-nah'rah): pasta sauced with pancetta, eggs, cheese, olive oil, and black pepper.

carciofo (kahr-chee'oh'-foh): artichoke.

carne (kahr'-neh): meat.

carota (kah-roh'-tah): carrot.

carpa/carpione (kahr'-pah/kahr-pee'oh'-neh): carp.

casa, della (kah'sah): in the style of the house.

casalinga (kah-sah-leen'-gah): homemade; in the style of the cook.

cassata (kahs-sah'-tah): molded Neapolitan ice cream with candied fruits and nuts.

cassata alla Siciliana (kahs-sah'-tah): a chocolate-iced sponge cake with candied fruit and sweetened ricotta cheese.

cavolfiore (kah-vohl-fee'oh'-ree): cauliflower.

cavolo (kah-voh'-loh): cabbage.

ceci (che'-chee): chickpeas.
cena (chen'-nah): supper.
cervello (cher-vehl'-loh): brains.
cervo (cher'-voh): venison.
cetriolo (cheh-tree-oh'-loh): cucumber.
cibo (chee'-boh): food.
ciliegia (chee-lee-eh'-jee'ah): cherry.
cipolla (chee-pohl'-lah): onion.
cocomero (koh-koh'-meh-roh): watermelon.
coda (koh'-dah): tail.
colazione (koh-lah-zee'oh'-neh): light meal—*prima colazione* is breakfast, *seconda colazione* is lunch.
compresso (kohm-preh'-soh): included.
con (kohn): with.
conchiglia (kohn-kee'-lee'ah): a shell-shaped pasta (literally, "shell").
condito (kohn-dee'-toh): seasoned; spiced.
coniglio (koh-nee'-lee'oh): rabbit.
coperto (koh-pehr'-toh): cover; cover charge.
coscia (koh'-schee'ah): leg; thigh.
costa / costata (koh'-stah / koh-stah'-tah): rib; rib steak.
costoletta (koh-stoh-leht'-tah): cutlet.
cotto (koht'-toh): cooked.
cozze (kohz'-zeh): mussel.
crescione (kreh-schee'oh'-neh): watercress.
crocchette (kroh-khet'-teh): croquette.
crostaceo (kroh-stah'-chee'oh): crustacean.
crostino (kroh-stee'-noh): crouton.
cuore (koo-oh'-reh): heart.
datteri (daht-teh'-ree): dates.
del / dell' / della / delle / dello (dehl / dehl / dehl'-lah / dehl'-leh / dehl'-loh): of the.
di (dee): of.
diavola, alla (dee-ah'-voh-lah): deviled.
ditali (dee-tah'-lee): very short pasta tubes (literally, "thimbles").
diverso (dee-vehr'-soh): a variety.
dolce (dohl'-cheh): sweet.
e (ee): and.
espresso (eh-sprehs'-soh): strong black coffee steam-brewed in a special machine.
fagiano (fah-jee'ah'-noh): pheasant.
fagioli (fah-jee'oh'-lee): beans.

farfalle (far-fah'-leh): a bow-shaped pasta (literally, "butterflies").

fatto (faht'-toh): made (as in "homemade").

fegato (feh'-gah-toh): liver.

fettucine (feht-too-chee'-neh): ¼-inch-wide ribbon noodles (literally, "small ribbons").

ferri, ai (fehr'-ree): grilled.

fico (fee'-koh): fig.

fisso (fees'-soh): fixed; set.

filletto (fee-leht'-toh): filet.

finocchio (fee-nohk'-kee-oh): fennel.

fiorentina, alla (fee-oh-rehn-tee'-nah): in the Florentine style or manner; often suggests the presence of spinach.

foglia (foh'-lee'ah): leaf.

formaggio (fohr-mahj'-jee'oh): cheese.

forno, al (fohr'-noh): oven-baked.

forte (fohr'-teh): strong.

fragole (frah'-goh-leh): strawberries.

freddo (frehd'-doh): cold.

fresco (frehs'-koh): fresh; cool.

frittata (freet-tah'-tah): omelette.

fritto (freet'-toh): fried.

frutta (froot'-tah): fruit.

fungo (foon'-goh): mushroom.

fusilli (foo-seel'-lee): corkscrewlike spaghetti (literally, "twist").

gallina (gahl-lee'-nah): hen.

gamberetto (gahm-beh-reht'-toh) small crayfish or shrimp.

gambero (gahm'-beh-roh): large crayfish.

gelato (geh-lah'-toh): ice cream.

ghiaccio (gee-ahch'-chee-oh): ice.

giorno, del (jee'ohr'-noh): of the day.

gli (lee): the.

gnocchi (n'yohk'-kee): dumplings.

granite (grah-nee'-teh): Italian ice (sherbetlike).

grasso (grahs'-soh): fat; fatty.

grissini (grees-see'-nee): thin bread sticks.

i/il (ee/eel: the.

in (een): in; into.

insalata (een-sah-lah'-tah): salad.

involtini (een-vohl-tee'-nee): rolled and stuffed thin pieces of veal or other meat.

la (lah): the.

lampone (lahm-poh'-neh): raspberry.

lasagna (lah-sah'-n'yah): a sauced and baked dish made with broad flat noodles.

latte (laht'-teh): milk.

lattuga (laht-too'-gah): lettuce.

le (lee): the.

legumi (leh-goo'-mee): vegetables.

lenticchie (lehn-teek'-kee'eh): lentils.

lepre (leh'-preh): hare.

lesso (lehs'-soh): boiled.

limone (lee-moh'-neh): lemon.

lingua (leen'-gwah): tongue.

linguini (leen-gwee'-nee): pasta resembling flattened spaghetti (literally, "small tongues").

lista (lees'-tah): menu.

litre (lee'-treh): liter.

lo (loh): the.

lombata (lohm-bah'-tah): loin.

lumaca (loo-mah'-kah): snail.

macaroni (mah-kah-roh'-nee): the umbrella term for tubular pasta (for example, ziti and elbows are macaroni; spaghetti is not).

macedonia (mah-cheh-doh'-nee-ah): mixed fruit or vegetables.

mafalde (mah-fahl'-deh): broad flat noodles with rippled edges.

magro (mah'-groh): lean.

maiale (mah-ee-ah'-leh): pork.

mandorla (mahn'-dohr-lah): almond.

manicotti (mah-nee-koht'-tee): stuffed tubular pasta baked in a sauce (literally, "little muffs").

manzo (mahn'-zoh): beef.

marinara, alla (mah-ree-nah'-rah): served with a sauce containing tomatoes, wine, garlic, herbs, and olive oil (literally, "in the sailor's style").

mela (meh'-lah): apple.

melanzana (meh-lahn-zah'-nah): eggplant.

melone (meh-loh'-neh): melon.

mezzo (mehz'zoh): half; middle.

merluzzo (mehr-looz'-zoh): hake.

midolla (mee-dohl'-lah): marrow.

miele (mee-eh'-leh): honey.

milanese (mee-lah-neh'-seh): coated with bread crumbs and fried (literally, "in the style of Milan").

minerale (mee-neh-rah'-leh): mineral.

minestra (mee-neh'-strah): soup.

minestrone (mee-neh-stroh'-neh): vegetable and pasta or rice soup.
misto (mee'-stoh): mixed.
mogliatelle (moh-lee'ah-tehl'-leh): sheep's testicles.
montone (mohn-toh'-neh): mutton.
mostarda (moh-stahr'-dah): mustard.
muscoli (moo-skoh'-lee): mussels.
naturale (nah-too-rah'-leh): cooked plain (literally, "natural").
nero (neh'-roh): black.
o (oh): or.
oca (oh'-kah): goose.
olio (oh'-lee-oh): oil.
oliva (oh-lee'-vah): olive.
oreganata (oh-reh-gah-nah'-tah): seasoned with oregano.
orzo (ohr'-zoh): rice-shaped pasta (literally, "barley").
osso (ohs'-soh): bone.
ostrica (oh'-stree-kah): oyster.
padella, in (pah-dehl'-lah): in the frying pan.
paesana, alla (pah-eh-zah'-nah): peasant style.
paese, del (pah-eh'-zeh): of the country.
pompelmo (pohm-pehl'-moh): grapefruit.
pancetta (pahn-cheht'-tah): a cured pork roll.
pane (pah'-neh): bread.
panna (pahn'-nah): cream.
parmigiana, alla (pahr-mee-jee'ah'-nah): cooked with grated Parmesan cheese.
pasta (pah'-stah): this umbrella term includes spaghetti (rod-shaped), macaroni (tubular), and noodles (ribbonlike).
pasta verde (pah'-stah vehr'-deh): green pasta, usually dyed with spinach.
pasticceria (pah-steech-cheh-ree'-ah): pastry.
pastini (pah-stee'-nee): soup-sized pasta.
pasto (pah'-stoh): meal.
patata (pah-tah'-tah): potato.
pepe (peh'-peh): pepper.
pera (peh'-rah): pear.
pesca (peh'-skah): peach.
pesce (pehs'-keh): fish.
pesto (peh'-stoh): a basil-based sauce.
petto (peht'-toh): breast.
piatto (pee-aht'-toh): dish.
piccante (peek-kahn'-teh): piquant; highly seasoned.

piccata (peek-kah'-tah): sautéed fillet, usually veal, flavored with lemon juice.

piccione (peech-chee-oh'-neh): pigeon.

piede (pee-eh'-deh): foot or trotter.

pignoli (pee-n'yoh'-lee): pine nuts.

piselli (pee-sehl'-lee): peas.

pizzaiola (peez-zah-ee-oh'-lah): covered with a sauce comprising tomatoes, garlic, olive oil, and oregano or other herbs.

polenta (poh-lehn'-tah): a cornmeal mush.

polipo/polpo (poh-lee'-poh/pohl'-poh): octopus.

polpette (pohl-peht'-teh): meatballs.

pollo (pohl'-loh): chicken.

pomodoro (poh-moh-doh'-roh): tomato.

porchetta (pohr-khet'-tah): roast suckling pig.

pranzo (prahn'-zoh): dinner; midday meal.

prezzemolo (prehz-zeh'-moh-loh): parsley.

prezzo (prehz'-zoh): price.

prima (pree'-mah): before.

primavera (pree'-mah-veh'-rah): the spring season.

primizie (pree-mee-zee'-eh): early fruits and vegetables.

primo (pree'-moh): first.

prugna (proo'-n'yah): plum.

prugna secca (proo'-n'yah sehk'-kah): prune.

punta (poon'-tah): point; tip.

puntino, cotto a (poon-tee'-noh, koht'-toh ah): cooked medium done (as with a steak).

quaglia (kwah'-lee'ah): quail.

quarto (kwahr'-toh): quarter; one-fourth.

radicchio (rah-deek'-kee'oh): a red-accented salad green.

ragu (rah-goo'): a rich, thick Bolognese sauce or stew.

rana (rah'-nah): frog.

rapa (rah'-pah): turnip.

ravanello (ra-vah-nehl'-loh): radish.

ravioli (rah-vee-oh'-lee): small stuffed pasta squares.

rigati (ree-gah'-tee): describes pasta that is grooved (as with ziti rigati).

ripieno (ree-pee'eh'-noh): stuffed.

risi e bisi (ree'-zee eh bee'-zee): a Venetian rice and pea combination.

riso (ree'-soh): rice.

risotto (ree-soht'-toh): a Milanese specialty—rice cooked and flavored with broth, wine, butter, saffron, etc.

rognone (roh-n'yoh'-neh): kidneys.
romana, alla (roh-mah-nah): in the Roman style or manner.
rosso (rohs'-soh): red.
rotelle (roh-tehl'lee): short thick corkscrewlike pasta (literally, "small wheels").
salato (sah-lah'toh): salted; salty.
sale (sah'leh): salt.
salsa (sahl'-sah): sauce.
saltimbocca (sahl-teem-bohk'kah): veal cutlet sautéed with ham and sage.
salvia (sahl'vee'ah): sage.
sangue, al (sahn'gweh): cooked rare (as with a steak).
sardina (sahr-dee'nah): sardine.
scaloppine (skah-lohp-pee'neh): small, thin slices of veal or other meat.
scampi (skahm'pee): prawn; word often misued for large shrimp.
secco (sehk'koh): dry.
seconda (seh-kohn'dah): second.
sedano (seh'dah-noh): celery.
selvaggina (sehl-vahj-jee'nah): game.
seme (seh'meh): seed.
semplice (sehm'plee-cheh): plain; simple.
senape (seh'nah-peh): mustard.
senza (sehn'zah): without.
seppia (sehp'-pee'ah): cuttlefish or squid.
servizio (sehr-vee'zee'oh): service.
sfogliatelle (sfoh-lee'ah-tehl'leh): a flaky pastry stuffed with sweetened ricotta cheese.
siciliana, alla (see-chee-lee'ah'nah): in the style or manner of Sicily.
sogliola (soh-lee'oh-lah): sole.
spaghetti (spah-geht'tee): thin rod-shaped pasta, not to be confused with macaroni, which are tubular, or noodles, which are flat. Literally, "lengthy string."
specialità (speh-chee'ah-lee-tah'): specialty.
spesso (spehs'soh): thick.
spezzatino (spehz-zah-tee'noh): cut into small pieces.
spiedino, al (spee-eh-dee'noh): cooked on a skewer.
spiedo, al (spee-eh'doh): cooked on a spit.
spinaci (spee-nah'chee): spinach.
spumone (spoo-moh'neh): frozen custardlike dessert.
sputino (spoo-tee'noh): snack.
stagione, di (stah-jee-oh'neh): in season.

stoccafisso (stohk-kah-fees′soh): dried cod.

stracciatella (strahk-chee′ah-tehl′lah): a curdled egg consommé flavored with grated cheese and semolina.

stracotto (strah-koht′toh): long-cooked; stewed.

stufato/stufatino (stoo-fah′toh/stoo-fah-tee′noh): stew.

su (soo): on; over.

succo (sook′koh): juice.

sugo (soo′goh): sauce; gravy.

suino (swee′noh): pork.

susina (soo-see′nah): plum.

tacchino (tahk-kee′noh): turkey.

tagliatelle (tah-lee′ah-tehl′leh): a broad noodle, slightly wider than fettuccine (stems from the verb "to cut").

tartaruga (tahr-tah-roo′gah): turtle.

tartufi (tahr-too′fee): truffles.

te (teh): tea.

tenero (teh-neh′roh): tender.

testa (teh′stah): head.

tonno (toh′noh): tuna.

tortellini (tohr-tehl-lee′nee): small stuffed ring-shaped pasta (literally, "small twists").

triglia (tree′lee'ah): mullet.

trippa (treep′pah): tripe.

tutta/tutto (too′tah/too′toh): everything; all; whole.

umido (oo-mee′doh): steamed; cooked in a liquid.

un/un'/una/uno (oon/oon/oo′-nah/oo′noh): a; an; one.

uova (oo'oh′vah): egg.

uva (oo′vah): grape.

vecchio (vehk′kee'oh): old.

verde (vehr′deh): green.

vermicelli (vehr-mee-chehl′lee): thin spaghetti (literally, "little worms").

vino (vee′noh): wine.

vongole (vohn-goh′leh): clams.

zabaglione (zah-bah-lee'oh′-neh): a dessert comprising whipped egg yolks, sugar, and Marsala.

zampone (zahm-poh′neh): pig's trotters stuffed with sausage.

ziti (zee′tee): large pasta tubes (literally, "bridegrooms").

zucchero (zook′keh-roh): sugar.

zuppa (zoop′pah): soup.

zuppa inglese (zoop′pah een-gleh′-seh): rum-soaked, custard-layered sponge cake.

10

Potpourri

As a well-rounded diner, you should also be conversant with these peripheral subjects and issues: "What's a Gourmet?"; "Are the Pleasures of the Table Sinful?"; "Exposing Food and Wine Snobs"; "The 'Pierre Must Be an Authority' Myth"; "So You Want to be a Restaurant Critic"; "Don't Envy a Restaurant Chef"; "The Pitfalls of Owning a Restaurant"; "How Sanitary Is Your Favorite Haunt?"; "Fast Foods"; "A Peek at the Future."

WHAT'S A GOURMET?

At a recent gourmet society dinner, a friend of mine remarked that she didn't particularly care for the truffle-stuffed squab. Overhearing her comment, a man sitting next to me confided: "Poor dear, she's probably just not used to this kind of food. But I can appreciate this squab. I'm a gourmet." As the meal progressed, I noticed that he seemed to be more impressed by the fact that the chef had shoved the delicacy "up the bird's rear end" than he was with more critical considerations. The baby pigeon happened to have been frozen, thawed, and overcooked, and it was served with an inappropriate, poorly prepared, lukewarm sauce. Black truffle or not, the squab was anything but a gourmet delight. I concluded that the man did not deserve the gastronomic title which he had bestowed upon himself.

Gourmet is one of the most abused words in the food lexicon. Over the past decades, snobs by the thousands have been adopting the label and thus have given the term a bad name. True gourmets love good eating and, though they are not necessarily experts, they know something about the cultivation, preparation, and presentation of food.

Most people confuse the word *gourmet* with other culinary titles. If a person's knowledge in the realm of food is convincingly broad and deep, and his or her appreciation of quality extremely keen, then you might call that individual an *epicure* (or *connoisseur*) rather than a gourmet. If this epicure also has a profound intellectual interest in food, then *gastronome* would be the correct appellation.

Gourmand, another tag, has two meanings: gourmet and glutton. Persons in the latter category prefer quantity to quality.

I have observed that a genuine gourmet compassionately responds to all sorts of sensory stimuli. Besides being able to detect the whetting cooking scents emanating from a small Romanian restaurant situated around the corner, he is quick to appreciate the song of the birds in his backyard and to spot the first monarch butterfly of the season.

Well-rounded gourmets have consuming interests beyond their bellies. At the dinner table they are able to discuss Einstein, El Greco, and Euripides with equal verve and savvy.

Some people who fancy themselves gourmets are really "special occasion" gourmets. They savor delectable foods at dinner parties and fine restaurants, but for the majority of their other meals they swallow a lot of commercially processed fare. True gourmets do not live by this double standard. If they are eating alone and having an omelette for breakfast, they want the omelette to be superlative.

The Roman general Lucius Licinius Lucullus exemplified this attitude. Lucullus, who habitually hosted luxurious banquets, one evening happened to be dining home alone. On that night, his servants prepared for him a less than grand meal. Lucullus sent it back and commanded his cooks to prepare him a more magnificent meal because, he remonstrated, "Tonight, Lucullus dines with Lucullus."

Every single offering at a gourmet's dinner is worthy of his or her palate. Never does a gourmet serve commercial mint jelly with roast leg of lamb, or a five-cent cigar with five-star cognac.

To a gourmet, the food and the camaraderie are always more important than the event. A New Orleans epicure, for instance, would probably enjoy eating at a good crayfish stand with a few friends more than dining at a five-hundred-dollar-a-plate black-tie gala dinner in the grand ballroom of an elegant hotel.

A food connoisseur relishes sharing conflicting opinions with fellow diners—and is not afraid to ask questions, even at the risk of seeming ignorant. Through such self-confidence comes augmented knowledge.

Finally, gourmets do not bore you with tedious gastronomic gabble at the dinner table. They know that such ramblings can ruin the appetite as surely as poorly cooked food. Downright tragedy occurs when a cook has prepared a memorable meal and the pseudogourmets open their mouths.

ARE THE PLEASURES OF THE TABLE SINFUL?

Practically every day I hear moral guardians denounce the pleasures of the table. To them, the gastronomic pursuit is selfish in light of the number of hungry people in our world. To me, these watchdogs have good intentions but lack a proper perspective.

Spending a reasonable amount of money on high-quality foods is no more sinful than, say, buying tennis rackets, stereo equipment, sports cars, or airline tickets for vacations in Europe. Fine foods are not vital as nutritional sources, but psychologists agree that a certain amount of self-indulgence is good for our mental health and may even prolong our lives.

Samuel Johnson championed gastronomic indulgence with these words:

> Some people have a foolish way of not minding, or pretending not to mind what they eat. For my part, I mind my belly very studiously, and very carefully; for I look upon it, that he who does not mind his belly will hardly mind anything else.

An Indonesian tribe, which apparently concurs with Dr. Johnson's sentiments, has a most delightful belief: Unless a tribesman treats his soul well by eating well, his soul will desert him. Thus, good fare literally becomes "soul food" in that part of the world.

Overindulgence is another matter. I do feel a sense of moral outrage whenever I hear of someone shelling out money on rare and costly food merely for the sake of extravagance. Conspicuous gastronomic consumption is not new. Petronius, in his *Satyricon,* tells us how the nouveaux riches of his day forked out small fortunes for ostentatious preparations like the tongues of songbirds.

In 1975, vehement letters deluged the desk of a *New York Times* food columnist after he described how he and a colleague had spent $4,000 on a thirty-one-dish, nine-wine dinner for two at Chez Denis in Paris. In fairness I should point out that thousands of other readers gained a vicarious thrill when they read about the once-in-a-lifetime wining and dining escapade, so more than the two participants gained value from the multi-thousand-dollar splurge.

Less than three years later, this modern record was broken by a couple at New York's Palace restaurant. Total outlay: $5,000 for two—including an $878 tip.

Japanese executives are notorious for their exorbitant eating exploits. As December rolls around each year, they give *bonen-kai* or "forget-the-year" parties where restaurant tabs routinely run into the hundreds or thousands of dollars. Amusing clients is a year-round activity, and many an executive has been admonished by his superior for failing to spend his full *kosai-hi* (entertaining budget). *Kosai-hi* is, as one Japanese manufacturer put it, "the lubricant that greases the nation's economy."

EXPOSING FOOD AND WINE SNOBS

By definition, food and wine snobs are pseudoexperts who flaunt their smattering of knowledge. Like vampires, they need victims—namely, us. Here's how to identify these dues-paying members of L'Académie de Snobberie de Cuisine.

One of the oldest ruses in the arsenal of pseudogourmets is to memorize a pocketful of facts without delving too deeply into the subject. For example, when confronted with a poached fillet of sole in a French restaurant, a snob will take a bite, then spout, "The chef cooked this fish in a liquid containing fish bones, thyme, parsley, chervil, bay leaf, butter, shallots, white wine, lemon juice, salt, pepper, as well as minced carrots, celery, and ham." All the snob is doing is reciting the fourteen flavoring agents that are most likely to be used in a fish fumet prepared by a textbook-trained Parisian chef.

This artifice can be played with many other cuisines as well. When an Indian curry dish is served, the counterfeit gourmet runs down a mental list of classic curry spices and sputters, "I perceive twenty-one distinct spices: cumin, cardamom, coriander seed, cinnamon, saffron, mace, nutmeg. . ."

With the existence of thorough reference books like Alexis Lichine's *Encyclopedia of Wines and Spirits,* it is easy for a person to feign wine connoisseurship merely by memorizing a lot of facts about one specific vineyard. This is what a young, mustached doctor obviously did the night before I met him at a wine tasting. After a brief exchange of hellos, he began his lengthy discourse on Château Grillet: "It's perched on the right bank of the Rhône River about fifty kilometers south of Lyons. Château Grillet is the smallest vineyard to have its own *appellation contrôlée.* Only about two hundred cases of this spicy, full-bodied wine are produced annually. The property is owned by . . ." The wine just happened to have been one of the preannounced featured wines of the evening. His monologue—it was certainly not a dialogue—left little to my imagination and even less to my patience. After his battery ran down, I was able (with a few quick questions) to ascertain beyond a shadow of a doubt that he knew little about wine beyond the confines of that particular vineyard. His answers (or the lack of them) suggested to me that he had never had a sip of Château Grillet before that night.

A variation of the "instant expert" game is to commit to memory the sixty-odd designated *crus* of the 1855 classification of the great red wines of Bordeaux. Snobs who use this ploy can respond to a query like "Have you tried Château Cos Labory?" with "I know it well—it carries a fifth-growth rating and comes from the commune of Saint-Estèphe." Names of vineyards glibly roll off their tongues, but with only superficial comprehension.

Another variation on the theme is for pseudoconnoisseurs to remember the taste qualities that wine experts customarily link with certain wines. They might, for instance, aver "smacks of black currants" whenever a Cabernet Sauvignon is served. They would declare "raspberries" for Zinfandel, "peachlike" for Chenin Blanc, "vegetal" for the wines produced in the Central Coast region of California, "apples" for quality Chardonnay, and probably "oaky" as well if that Chardonnay came from a Californian boutique winery. If these oenological quacks know that their audience are babes in arms when it comes to wine, they use whatever associations come to mind, just as long as they keep straight faces.

Snobs use menus as vehicles for name dropping. As their eyes come to rest on the *billi-bi* listing, they mumble, "I prefer this soup in Chez Dolle because its mussels come from Gaston Cove." While glowering at the wine list, they whisper, "I don't think we should order this 1974 Saint-Joseph. When I tasted this particular vintage in Lasserre in Paris with Count de Valera, it had a prounounced *goût de terroir*."

Some snobs claim they can pinpoint the vintage and vineyard of nearly every wine they sample in a blind tasting. No one—not even Sir Dionysus Bacchus—could perform this feat with repeated success unless the individual restricts his or her expertise to a fairly limited number of the world's five-thousand-plus distinct wines. When charlatans are confronted with a concealed label at a blind tasting, they try to lower the odds against them by using tricks, such as getting to the event early to sneak a peek at the shipping list or, once the wines are on the table, noting the shape and color of the bottles. (Example: Though Mosel and Rheingau wines both come in tall, narrow-neck bottles, the container of the first is green and that of the second, brown.)

Not surprisingly, I have met few professional wine buyers who engage in wine-identification contests. And those who participate in the competitions perform more poorly than most people would suspect, because the buyers are not trained for blind tastings. In their daily work they insist on knowing beforehand the vineyard and vintage of a wine as it sits in the barrel or bottle. This makes sense because when you are responsible for determining whether a wine is a sound commercial investment, you need to eliminate all the unnecessary guesswork.

Self-delusion is epidemic among some snobs. They believe they know practically everything there is to know about food and wine. Nonsense. There is so much to know about wining and dining that it would take at least twenty-five lifetimes for anyone to master this subject. At the University of California at Davis, you can spend four years gaining a B.S. degree in oenology alone. Learning about food and wine can be a frustrating process: the more you know, the more paltry your knowledge seems compared to the wealth of information which exists on the subject. So be suspicious when someone boasts of sweeping gastronomic knowledge. Remember Touchstone's advice in Shakespeare's *As You Like It:* "The fool doth think he is wise, but the wise man knows himself to be a fool."

I know many snobs who behave as if they are born gourmets. No one comes into this world with a gourmet's palate. The ability to detect distinctions in quality is largely an acquired skill. When you were three years old, for instance, you wouldn't have been able to appreciate the difference between a superb and a merely good hamburger any more than you would have been able to note the virtuosity gap between a great and a merely good impressionist painter.

Some snobs jump to the conclusion that if they are knowledgeable about wine, they must be experts on food as well. I frequently see self-proclaimed gourmets fastidiously sniffing their wine while neglecting to evaluate and appreciate their food with the same care. *Inconsistency* is the word to describe this behavior.

Many people consider themselves connoisseurs simply because they are members of a gourmet society. Membership in a food and wine club does not automatically a gourmet make.

Don't get me wrong. I have no objections to gourmet societies per se. Almost every club that I've visited has its own contingent of members who are gourmets in the original sense of the word. Moreover, programs at events can sometimes be exciting and educational. When a committee assembles a battery of hard-to-find wines for a tasting, the result is particularly valuable.

The principal bone I have to pick with gourmet societies is that a fair proportion of their members shouldn't be members. They join because membership has social cachet. These misfits tend to be pretentious bores; they take themselves too seriously and know less about gastronomy than they would have us believe.

Gourmet organizations are natural breeding grounds for snobs because, as is the case in the fields of art and music, a sprinkling of knowledge is usually sufficient to constitute a facade of connoisseurship. North Carolina's motto, *esse quam videri* ("to be rather than to seem"), has limited relevancy among the highfalutin members. Instead of aspiring to share opinions and information, these members too often try to impress each other with their imagined credentials and past experiences. You can sometimes cut with a butter knife the tension created in the competitive environment.

Another type of snob who erroneously assumes the mantle of authority is the diner who thinks he is qualified to be a bona fide food critic just because he has dined out on the average of ten times a week for the past twenty years. Unquestionably, a person with that kind of restaurant exposure would have accumulated a great deal of restaurant-going savvy. Nevertheless, the experience by itself is not a sufficient qualification. This person's presumptions remind me of the man who recently claimed that he would make a great television critic for a major daily newspaper because he had watched thirty-nine thousand hours of TV in a decade.

Snobs are intolerant and are apt to make comments like "How could anyone not adore caviar?" or "Only French [or California] wines are great." In matters of food, there is room for disagreement—each person's sensory mechanisms are physically different from his or her neighbor's. Debates will always exist, even among the world's foremost gastronomic experts. As the Roman poet and philosopher Lucretius wrote, "What is food to one man may be fierce poison to others."

To some snobs, if a dish isn't delicate, it isn't quality. Delicacy is not always the hallmark of culinary excellence—many a robust peasant dish is more worthy of an educated palate than are bland concoctions that are meted out at lackluster luxury restaurants.

Snobs are afflicted with verbal diarrhea. They feel compelled to volunteer their opinion on everything they happen to taste—and when all is said and done, they keep on saying it. Not every food deserves critical comment. Unless the item is notably good or bad, diners should keep their mouths shut.

Snobs' culinary judgments are usually couched in a sardonic tone. Like H. L. Mencken's cynic, a snob is "a man who, when he smells flowers, looks around for the coffin." One reason for a snob's faultfinding penchant is that criticism generally requires fewer supporting facts and less logical development than does praise. Also, a critical posture is more conducive to wit and puts most opponents on the defensive.

Whenever you encounter snobs, don't debate them. They thrive on polemic nourishment. I have discovered through the years that the best defense against snobs is to ignore them. But be forewarned; this tactic might make them fume, for it fans the flames of their insecurity.

THE "PIERRE MUST BE AN AUTHORITY" MYTH

I often hear comments similar to "Pierre says it is the best French restaurant in San Francisco. You can trust his judgment because, after all, he's French." This reasoning is flawed.

Obviously, the average Frenchman knows vastly more about French cuisine than does the average American. One should not, however, deduce from this fact that all French citizens have a profound understanding of their native cuisine. Nor should one conclude that the average Frenchman in our country is more qualified to judge a French restaurant than are thousands of American gourmets who have been avidly cooking and eating first-rate French food at home and abroad for years. Run-of-the-mill French expatriates too often derive their authority from their Gallic accent.

The idiotic myth that a Frenchman is automatically well informed about French food is far more prevalent in America than in England, Germany, or Italy. The typical citizen of one of these European countries travels to France more often than does his American counterpart and is therefore more attuned to how the average Frenchman of today cooks and eats. Irrefutable evidence of the steady demise of the palates of numerous Frenchmen is provided by the *supermarchés* which are now mushrooming all over France. Every day millions of Frenchmen (a small but significant and burgeoning share of the population of France) stream into these emporiums—the Gallic equivalents of American supermarkets—and buy canned and frozen foods galore. *Alors!*

Americans are quick to assign nonexistent gastronomic expertise to other foreign expatriates as well. How often I have heard: "This must be a superb Chinese restaurant—every diner here is Chinese." Certainly some Chinese are gastronomic illiterates, while some non-Chinese have acquired a fair understanding of Chinese cuisine. Take me. I'm the first to admit that I'm more ignorant about Chinese cuisine than are the majority of Chinese, but I do know that I've given lessons on how to prepare a few Cantonese dishes to second- and third-generation Chinese-Americans whose forebears had emigrated from Canton. During a culinary visit to Peking, I was allowed to cook a stir-fried shrimp dish in a restaurant. None of the Chinese in the dining room who ate and apparently enjoyed my dish suspected that a Westerner had cooked it. Personally, I thought I prepared the speciality well enough that I did not have to apologize for my exploits, though I have to admit that the difference between my version and that of the restaurant's master chef was like night and day.

SO YOU WANT TO BE A RESTAURANT CRITIC

Being a restaurant critic is not all peaches and cream. Before you quit your present job and accept the "utopian" post at your local newspaper, you should be aware of the occupational liabilities you face. Let me tell you some of them.

Don't be surprised if fewer people invite you to dinner. Home cooks become paranoid, fearing that you will detect flaws and openly criticize their culinary triumphs. This apprehension is usually unjustified, because most home cooks I know serve far better food than is offered in the typical restaurant.

If you are going to make a fair critique of a restaurant, you will have to taste the bad along with the good—and, believe me, there is far more bad than good in most restaurants. Let us assume that you learn by word of mouth that the veal stew at some local establishment is horrendous. As a diner eating solely for pleasure, you would avoid that dish or, possibly, the restaurant altogether. As a critic, you would have to sample the dish to make the judgment firsthand.

Maintaining your anonymity is essential. Doing it, however, is not always easy, and sometimes it has created embarrassing problems for me. More than once I've made a reservation under an assumed name only to forget the pseudonym when I arrived at the restaurant (I now restrict my choices to the name of my guest, or to one of my three well-memorized anonyms). In my endeavor not to blow my cover, I surreptitiously write my notes on small slips of paper, but, as it sometimes occurs, I can't decipher my scribblings the next morning. Once I dictated my notes to a miniature microphone concealed in my lapel, but I quickly gave up that device when I noticed that the people at the adjoining table were obviously thinking that I was one of those psychotics who talk to themselves in public places. Another time I wore a wig to disguise myself, but I scratched that idea from my repertoire when I spotted odd hairs falling into my soup.

If you think restaurant critics are nit-picking and cruelly unfair, you should hear how they are maligned behind their backs at cocktail parties. Not even the best of the restaurant reviewers is immune to the outrageous slings and arrows of restaurant-goers who know far less about gastronomy than do the experts. Yet these critic loathers faithfully read reviews because of, in part, the safety factor. If the reader is taking someone to an untried restaurant that a critic recommended and it turns out to be as touted, he can pat himself on the back in front of his friend for having the wisdom to dine there. If the experience turns out to be disappointing, for whatever reasons, the blame for visiting the restaurant may be placed on the shoulders of the reviewer—a most convenient scapegoat.

Restaurateurs, too, seldom have kind words to say about the critics. I've heard irate owners inveigh against "those eat and pan fiends who hide behind the protection of the First Amendment." "Why," they ask, "do publishers hire critics to pick on restaurants and not on TV repair shops and used-car lots?" "Why should critics be allowed to inflate their egos at the expense of people who have their life savings invested in restaurants?" "Since a critic's role demands that he be picayune," one restaurant owner asked, "how can he experience my restaurant like my typical customer?" These are good questions for which there are no easy answers except that quality restaurant criticism does benefit the public at large. Moreover, restaurants should not take the judgment of an impartial critic as a personal attack. As the nineteenth-century philosopher Nietzsche remarked:

Insects sting not in malice, but because they want to live. It is the same with critics; they desire our blood, not our pain.

Some restaurateurs do not take the condemnation of the critics lying down. A number retaliate by placing nasty ads next to the reviewer's weekly column. Others have instigated multimillion-dollar libel suits against some of my colleagues. More than one restaurateur has threatened to punch me in the nose or to instruct the Mafia to give me cement shoes and dump me in the East River. Who said reviewing restaurants was an enviable job?

DON'T ENVY A RESTAURANT CHEF

Most people have a romantic notion of the workaday life of a chef—and they don't even know that there's a profound difference between being a cook and a chef. Cooks prepare food at home on a small scale for those dear to them. Chefs are mass feeders—they prepare meals in restaurants for scores, hundreds, and sometimes thousands of strangers.

If cooks can't find good pork in the market, they switch to veal. This option is not open to chefs in a restaurant with standard deliveries and printed menus.

Unlike cooks, chefs have little opportunity to be creative. Customers complain if they don't prepare favorite dishes the same way time after time.

While cooks work for limited hours in the comforts of their homes, chefs labor all day in hot, noisy, and relatively messy kitchens. Of the nation's one million professional chefs, only ten thousand make a decent living. Chefs who earn more than a thousand dollars a week can fit into the kitchen of the 21 Club.

History tells of a seventeenth-century French chef named Vatel who committed suicide when his fish supply for one of Louis XIV's banquets wasn't delivered on schedule. Let his demise be a lesson to all would-be chefs.

THE PITFALLS OF OWNING A RESTAURANT

A proprietor said to me in jest, "Running your own restaurant is like playing poker: you must be sufficiently intelligent to beat your competitors but not so intelligent that you get bored with the routine." I have so much sympathy for my friends who are restaurateurs that I emphatically discourage any of my other friends who express even the slightest interest in entering the wining and dining business. I'm not normally a pessimist, but there are simply too many trials and tribulations that accompany restaurant ownership.

The initial investment is high, and your operating costs—rent, food, and labor—will certainly spiral upward. Even if you are successful, the odds are your business won't last more than ten years.

You need special skill and talent, including old-fashioned showmanship and modern business management. You'll have to be on constant guard lest your employees rob you blind, or your suppliers deliver substandard merchandise at inflated prices. You'll face labor troubles galore—the unions can shackle you with petty work rules, and your chef might walk out on Saturday night at the drop of a *toque blanche*. Even worse, the chef might show up tipsy or not at all.

"The boys" from your local organized-crime family will probably insist that you subscribe to their linen and carting service and that you allow them to install their cigarette machines. When you fail to comply, you could get a veiled arson threat. To make matters worse, the local government will harass you with an entanglement of regulations.

The hours are long and wrong. When your friends are partying on Friday and Saturday nights, you'll be working.

Customers who know little about food will inevitably criticize your cuisine; when finished dining, they depart with expensive silver souvenirs. You'll, of course, have to pander to obnoxious (but rich) drunks who think being boisterous is their birthright. Finally, after all this, some incompetent critic can walk in and pan your baby.

So, if you still want to open a restaurant, courageous soul, be my guest. You must just end up lucky—and be one of the restaurateurs who are both successful and still love the work.

HOW SANITARY IS YOUR FAVORITE HAUNT?

When it comes to sanitary conditions in a restaurant, one should never take to heart poet Thomas Gray's advice: "Where ignorance is bliss, 'tis folly to be wise."

Some municipalities require that restaurants post (or otherwise make available to the public) the most recent results of their inspection by the health department. Because a restaurant has not been cited for a violation, it does not necessarily imply a clean bill of health. Many restaurants that should be closed down are not shuttered because there are too few inspectors in big-city health departments to give proper scrutiny to all the eating establishments.

Most of the health inspectors are dedicated and honest chaps who work hard for little money. Sadly, there are also those dishonest inspectors who, for the price of a twenty- or fifty-dollar bill, will overlook rat droppings, scurrying roaches, buzzing flies, moldy foods, grimy pipes, filthy pantries, malfunctioning refrigerators, tepid dishwashing water, dirty fingernails, festering hand sores, and whatever else could cause you to become sick from a food-borne disease like salmonella or staphylococcus.

Lest I scare you away from the wonderful world of restaurant dining, permit me to emphasize that sanitary conditions in your better restaurants are fairly good, and are superior to those in millions of homes. Some restaurants are unjustly blamed for sins they never committed. For instance, I hosted an Indian banquet and one of my guests got sick the next day. He shook an accusing finger at the restaurant. Interestingly, of the eight people who attended that dinner, only he became indisposed. We had all eaten the same food and the same quantity—the only apparent difference was that he drank heavily that night.

FAST FOODS

Our nation has more than one hundred thousand fast-food outlets, one for every two thousand Americans. McDonald's alone has more than five thousand cloned operations grossing about ten billion dollars annually. Indeed, the commerce of fast foods is big business.

Whether the chain specializes in hamburgers, roast beef sandwiches, Southern fried chicken, fish and chips, tacos, or pizza, its
outlets seem to be created more as marketing formulas than
places to eat. The chains' ten-ingredient recipe for success seems
to be:

     low prices
     limited menu selection
     predictability (no surprises)
     high volume
     high-traffic location
     fast customer turnover
     appeal to all age groups
     low wages (hire teenagers)
     self-service
     contrived decor

Decorating is an exact science with big fast-food chains. The
goal is not only to lure you inside their premises but also to hasten
your departure in order to make room for another customer. This
is especially true in fast-paced business districts. (A counter eatery in Rockefeller Center once boasted a turnover of nearly ten
people per stool during the 11:00 A.M. to 2:00 P.M. lunch period.)

The color scheme often comprises vivid contrasting hues such
as reds, purples, yellows, and oranges because they produce an
unsettling psychophysiological effect. Unconsciously, you want
to rush your meal and leave. Brilliant lights produce the same
results.

Other antilingering measures include installing molded plastic
chairs that are a shade or two short of being comfortable.
Whenever possible, the temperature is kept low (around 60°F.) to
discourage you from removing your coat. Should you shed it, you
may discover that coat racks are insufficient or nonexistent.

High rent is not the only reason why seating is cramped. You
are not apt to tell your life story to your companion if you are
practically sitting on the lap of the stranger next to you.

Coffee and soup are sometimes not as hot as they should be.
This way, you won't have to wait several minutes for the liquid to
cool.

Jukeboxes generally don't exist in fast-food outlets. The last
thing most fast-food operators want is for their eateries to be

turned into hangouts with idle teenagers hogging precious table space.

Service in many fast-food operations is deliberately slackened during the nonstandard eating hours. Instead of opening another cash register station when a line begins to lengthen, a manager will force you to wait. The queue makes the eatery seem popular and gives a message to insecure passersby that it is socially permissible to be seen eating at that hour.

Nutrition is a controversial issue in the world of fast foods. Is the fare they serve junk food? The answer is a qualified yes. On the plus side is the pizza—a quality specimen offers you a fair balance of proteins, carbohydrates, and fats. Specialties such as hamburgers, fish cakes, and chicken pieces are somewhat wholesome, but regrettably they have too many calories for the amount of nutrition they provide. A Burger King Whopper with cheese, for instance, has a whopping total of 740 calories—and that doesn't include the roughly 400 calories for the customary side order of cola and french fries. Moreover, the normally nutritious fries are frequently oversalted—as is virtually everything else served in fast-food outlets. Yet I doubt fast food will cause your body any harm if you eat the fare only occasionally and shun the blatant junk foods such as shakes and pies.

Fast-food fare is boringly repetitious. The difference between the offerings in one outlet and its competitor across the street is often a matter of presentation and marketing positioning rather than content.

Quality and fast foods have never been synonymous terms in my lexicon. Nearly all the food served in these filling stations is mediocre or worse, racked with culinary shortcomings: pressed-meat burgers with soggy lettuce; greasy fried chicken with dry interiors; bland fish cakes with mushy textures; gristly roast beef sandwiches on stale bread; doughy pizzas topped with soapy cheese; stale tacos stuffed with gooey fillings; oily french fries with decay spots; prefabricated chemical shakes without the ice cream. Millions enjoy this caliber of excellence because they have grown accustomed to it. If they had a high standard of what certain foods should taste like, the fast-food industry would go into an economic nose dive.

A PEEK AT THE FUTURE

The restaurant-going public will become increasingly polarized.

At one pole, there will be the vast majority of Americans. They will consume blander, junkier, and more processed foods than ever before. I wish I could paint a rosier picture, but anyone who denies this accelerating trend need only observe what's happening at the typical eating establishments around the country. H. L. Mencken's statement "No one ever went broke underestimating the taste of the American people" is becoming ever more valid.

At the other pole will be roughly 5 percent of the American public. This percentage may seem small, but it amounts to more than ten million people who will be insisting on quality foods. Their multibillion-dollar buying clout will be sufficient to ensure the availability of enough quality restaurants for those who care. To these lovers of first-rate foods, I dedicate my book.

About the Author

Howard Hillman passionately loves to dine out. He has eaten in the best (and some of the worst) establishments in more than one hundred countries around the world, from France to China. He has rated restaurants for America's largest newspaper, the *New York News,* and has written dining-out guidebooks to major American cities.

His other books include *Great Peasant Dishes of the World* (Houghton Mifflin), *The Cook's Book* (Avon), *Kitchen Science* (Houghton Mifflin), *The Book of World Cuisines* (Penguin), *The Diner's Guide to Wines* (Hawthorn), and *The Gourmet Guide to Beer* (Washington Square Press).

Hillman's books have been critically praised, selected by book clubs, and designated Outstanding Reference Books by both the American Library Association and the *Library Journal.*

His articles have been published in the *New York Times,* the *Washington Post,* the *Chicago Tribune,* the *Wall Street Journal, Newsweek, Self, Cook's Magazine,* and *Food & Wine,* among other periodicals.

Howard Hillman lectures on food and wine, and is a frequent guest on radio and TV talk shows. When he is not eating, cooking, or traveling, he can usually be found perusing his extensive food and wine reference library.

He is a Harvard Business School graduate. Hillman's general background includes the presidency of the National Academy of Sports and a vice-presidency of the American Film Theatre. He is a quality control consultant to major corporations.